CONFIDENTIALITY IN THE UNITED STATES

A Legal and Canonical Study

Donna Krier Ioppolo
Marie Breitenbeck, O.P.
Elissa A. Rinere, C.P.
Ronald P. Stake

CANON LAW SOCIETY OF AMERICA
Washington, D.C. 20064

ISBN: 0-943616-43-3
SAN: 237-6296

TABLE OF CONTENTS

Introduction
James A. Coriden 1

Civil Law and Confidentiality: Implications for the Church
Donna Krier Ioppolo 3

Appendix: Statutes and Court Decisions of the Fifty States
Donna Krier Ioppolo 49

The Canonical Tradition of Confidentiality Pertaining to Oral Communications
Marie Breitenbeck, O.P. 93

The Confidentiality of Written Documents in Canon Law
Elissa A. Rinere, C.P. 125

Grounding the "Priest-Penitent Privilege" in American Law
Ronald P. Stake 145

Addendum on Policy Making
Marie Breitenbeck, O.P. 163

Contributors to *Confidentiality* 167

INTRODUCTION

This book deals with the timely and sensitive issue of confidential communications in American law and in the canon law of the Roman Catholic church. Recent court cases and legislation, such as that relating to child abuse, have focused attention on the issue of access to oral and written communications of church personnel. When can a priest be compelled to testify in court? When must diocesan records be handed over? Who is obligated to report a suspected crime? The present state of the civil law and of the church's own discipline on these and related questions is the subject of this study.

In the lead article Donna Krier Ioppolo, Program Director at DePaul University Law School's Center for Church/State Studies, sets out the current legal situation and addresses four central questions: 1) Who is bound by the "clergy privilege"? 2) What communications are covered by the "clergy privilege"? 3) What are the limitations on the privilege? 4) How can confidentiality be better protected? A substantial bibliography of writings on legal issues of confidentiality and clergy malpractice provides direction for further study of these important questions.

This article is key to understanding and evaluating the analysis of statutes and court decisions of each of the fifty states, which follows in an appendix.

The study then turns to the canon law of the church. Marie Breitenbeck, O.P., Judge of the Court of Appeals for the Province of Atlanta, presents the canonical tradition on *oral* communications. She begins with the seal of confession and then treats the secrecy required of various church officials such as consultors, nominators, chancery officials, religious superiors and tribunal personnel. The present canonical norms are clearly set forth and a select bibliography is appended.

Elissa Rinere, C.P., Judge of the Archdiocesan Tribunal of Hartford, writes on the confidentiality of *written* documents in canon law. She treats the various levels of access and confidentiality appropriate to parish and diocesan archives and to tribunal records. The rules of the present Code of Canon Law are examined in the light of earlier church legislation.

Ronald Stake, a presbyter of the Archdiocese of Chicago who is also an attorney, studies the "priest-penitent privilege" in sacramental history, in English law, and as it developed in American law. He reflects on the application of the privilege to non-priests, and its limitation by mandatory reporting statutes. Stake concludes his article with evidence that the privilege is based on First Amendment "free exercise" grounds.

A brief addendum on policy-making within the church concludes the volume.

This study resulted from the cooperative efforts of the Canon Law Society of America Committee on Civil Law and Canon Law and the Center for Church/State Studies of DePaul University's College of Law. It was suggested by William Schumacher, Judicial Vicar of the Court of Appeals of the Province of Chicago, after he heard Donna Krier's presentation on confidential communications to the Midwest Canon Law Society Convention in April, 1987. The Canon Law Society Committee, whose members were Peter M. Shannon, Jordon Hite, T.O.R., and I, approved the idea and pursued it. We sought and received the collaboration of the Center, especially in the person of Donna Krier Ioppolo, and we searched out the other authors. They graciously offered their generous and learned assistance.

The Committee is very proud of this study. We express our profound gratitude to everyone who contributed to it and to the members and leaders of the Canon Law Society of America who made it possible.

We hope that this book will stimulate and aid in the development of appropriate policies in dioceses and religious communities. May this study of the law and canons on confidential communications contribute to the church's more effective witness and ministry in the United States.

James A. Coriden
February 1, 1989 — Washington Theological Union

Civil Law and Confidentiality

DONNA KRIER IOPPOLO

I. INTRODUCTION

While the concept of confidentiality in communications made to priests is an ancient and essential element in the Catholic Church, the concept has not fared quite so well in the civil[1] courts of the United States. Two factors have played a role in the development of the priest-penitent or clergy privilege statutes: constitutional requirements set forth in the First Amendment and the general rules of evidence. The analysis of these statutes is complicated by the fact that the evidentiary rules of privilege can differ from state to state.

A. Constitutional Requirements

The religion clauses of the First Amendment to the United States Constitution[2] have been interpreted to mean, among other things, that all religions must be treated equally. No religion and no religious practice can be given favored status. While this provision has generally worked to the benefit of all faith groups, it has made the discussion of confidential communications in religious settings quite complex.

The Catholic Church sets forth its demand for secrecy in the *Code of Canon Law*[3] which establishes the "seal of confession." Confessors are bound not to reveal in any way what has been told to them in confession and the penalties for violation are most

[1]In the context of this article, "civil" courts and "civil" law will be used to refer to the statutes and proceedings of the United States government or those of the various states as opposed to canon law, the law of the Catholic Church. Civil law includes both civil and criminal actions.

[2]"Congress shall make no law respecting an establishment of religion or prohibiting the free exercise thereof...."

[3]Canon 983.

severe.[4] Constitutional decisions by the United States Supreme Court which require the government to defer to church law and not interfere with the practice of religion demand that the seal of confession be accorded great respect.

However, few other religious bodies raise the rite of reconciliation (or confession) to the sacramental level. While the clergy of other traditions are bound to preserve the confidences which come to them in their respective forms of pastoral counseling, the seal of confession with its penalty of excommunication for violation does not exist in these traditions. Consequently, while it would be quite easy for civil courts to acknowledge the sacramental seal and preserve confidentiality in cases where it applies, it would be unconstitutional to grant this privilege to a single religious body and not to others. Likewise, if clergy of all faith traditions are to be accorded a privilege to preserve confidential communications made to them in settings other than confession, then the privilege must be extended to the Catholic clergy for these forms of pastoral counseling as well.

B. General Rules of Evidence

The statutes regarding the clergy privilege are found as part of each state's law of evidence. The fundamental rule is "that the public ... has a right to every man's evidence."[5] This duty to "disclose all that is needed for the ascertainment of truth applies to every form and material of evidence whatever. In particular it applies to such evidential material as exists in a person's hands in the form of documents."[6] Privileges, including the clergy privilege, are an exception to the general rule that all evidence relevant to a case must be made public.

> (F)our fundamental considerations are recognized as necessary to the establishment of a privilege against the disclosure of communications:
>
> (1) The communications must originate in a *confidence* that they will not be disclosed.
>
> (2) This element of *confidentiality must be essential* to the full and satisfactory maintenance of the rela-

[4]Canon 1388.

[5]8 Wigmore, *Evidence*, sec. 2192 (McNaughton rev. 1961 and Supp. 1988).

[6]8 Wigmore, *Evidence*, sec. 2193, (McNaughton rev. 1961 and Supp. 1988).

tion between the parties.

(3) The *relation* must be one which in the opinion of the community ought to be sedulously *fostered.*

(4) The *injury* that would inure to the relation by the disclosure of the communications must be *greater than the benefit* thereby gained for the correct disposal of the litigation.[7]

The relationship between clergy and their communicants had been recognized as one of those essential relationships that ought to be fostered by society. It is apparent that the counseling done by clergy is an important part of this relationship and communicants would not feel free to bare their souls if that communication were not undertaken in an atmosphere of confidence.

Because of these fundamental considerations, the clergy privilege has been recognized in some form by all fifty states. And yet, it is often apparent that the best evidence in a case may reside with a member of the clergy. Attorneys and judges will often press hard to get the evidence necessary to bring a case to a successful conclusion.

Recently, public policy has shifted in a number of areas so that injury to the relationship between clergy and communicants is no longer seen as great as the benefit gained by the public in having cases correctly and completely resolved. One area of heightened concern has been the abuse and neglect of children. Many states have restricted the application of the clergy privilege in these matters to foster the safety of children.

C. Our Federal System of Government

Under the system of government in the United States, laws can be enacted by both the Congress and by each of the fifty state legislatures. Although rules of evidence do exist for federal trials, these rules do not include the clergy privilege. Instead, these rules "shall be determined in accordance with State law."[8] Consequently, discussion of the law of clergy privilege must in reality include all fifty statutes which contain this privilege.

[7]8 Wigmore, *Evidence,* sec. 2285, (McNaughton rev. 1961 and Supp. 1988).
[8]Federal Rules of Evidence, Rule 501.

Furthermore, statutes do not stand alone, but are affected by the interpretation of the courts. States differ in how broadly or narrowly the privilege statutes are to be interpreted and their provisions applied. Consequently, identically worded statutes may yield different results in different states depending upon judicial decisions.

In the final analysis, clergy privilege statutes are unique to each state. A general discussion of the theory of the clergy privilege and the ways in which it has been applied are not of much use to clergy facing a particular circumstance in a specific jurisdiction. All clergy, and all those practicing ministry under whatever title, must be aware of the limits of the clergy privilege in their state and how it applies to them in the various activities in which they are engaged.

While this article will approach the clergy privilege on a general level, the individual minister will find the most value in the appendix which contains a detailed analysis of each state statute. The article will make an overall analysis of the components of clergy privilege and discuss the variety of limitations placed upon it and is intended to expand upon and explain the specifics given in the appendix. The discussion will include 1) who is bound by the clergy privilege; 2) what communications are covered by the privilege including oral communications and documents; 3) what are the limits placed on the privilege; and 4) what steps can be taken to improve the civil law on confidentiality and the Church's internal policies which govern such matters. Readers are encouraged to make constant reference to the analysis of their own state statute while reading this article to determine how the general analysis applies.

The appendix to this article with the state-by-state analysis of the clergy privilege statutes was constructed between May 1 and August 31, 1988, generally in alphabetical order. Changes are being made to these statutes with some frequency; those changes not *published* by September 1 are not included in this analysis.[9] Even the best statutory analysis, however, cannot serve as a

[9]In the statutory citations I noted the date of the state's current statutory supplement volume available and consulted for statutory changes and court decisions. Analysis is applicable through that volume.

substitute for direct legal advice. Should anyone encounter a problem, particularly if a subpoena has been served, an attorney must be consulted at once.

This article is written primarily for a Roman Catholic audience in its use of terminology for kinds of ministries and pastoral activities, and particularly in relation to the interaction between civil and canon law. While state statutes and the analyses which appear in the appendix clearly relate to clergy of all traditions, the explanations given here, while not limited to the Catholic context, should be read in that light.

II. WHO IS BOUND BY THE CLERGY PRIVILEGE?

In the struggle to make clergy privilege statutes inclusive of all faith traditions, these statutes use an extensive variety of terms to describe who is to be covered under them. This list includes, among others, minister, priest, rabbi, clergyman, accredited Christian Science practitioner, religious practitioner, and minister of the gospel. Statutes limiting the privilege to "any Christian or Jewish minister by whatever name called"[10] or a minister "of an established church"[11] or "of an established and legally cognizable church"[12] may be unconstitutional as not inclusive of the clergy of traditions more recently appearing in the United States. Many statutes refer to duly licensed, ordained or consecrated ministers and one defines this as those "authorized to perform a marriage ceremony"[13] within the jurisdiction. Some states limit the statute further to persons who devote "a substantial portion of (their) time" to the service of a religious organization[14] or that the clergyman be "settled in the work of ministry."[15]

A caveat which cannot be too strongly emphasized is that the word "minister" should not be interpreted to include all those who engage in ministry. In the last twenty years a plethora of ministries

[10]Georgia.

[11]Kentucky, Maryland, Pennsylvania, North Carolina.

[12]Ohio.

[13]District of Columbia.

[14]Alabama.

[15]Connecticut.

have appeared in the Catholic Church, many undertaken by the laity, carrying titles such as youth minister, campus minister, pastoral minister, etc. The appearance of the word "minister" in a job title does not necessarily qualify a person for coverage under a privilege statute, and more often than not these lay ministers will not be covered.

An attempt was made to define the term "minister" in the context of a federal Selective Service exemption case.[16] The court determined that a "duly ordained minister"

> is one who has followed a prescribed course of study of religious principles, has been consecrated to the service of living and teaching that religion through an ordination ceremony under the auspices of an established church, has been commissioned by that church as its minister in the service of God, and generally is subject to control or discipline by a council of the church by which he was ordained.[17]

The court further held that only these ministers were exempt "and not those consecrated laymen happily found in the membership of every church who live and serve well."[18]

The key idea the privilege statutes attempt to express is that "clergy" are considered those duly licensed, commissioned or ordained by a religious body and subject to the laws of that body. In the Catholic context this would include bishops, priests, and permanent and transitional deacons. Because some statutes limit the scope of the privilege to confessions made according to the discipline of the religious body (see the following section), the extent to which deacons are covered may be limited in some jurisdictions.

It can generally be assumed that Catholic priests are covered to the extent the law allows when they are engaged in their religious ministry. That may not be true when they serve in other roles. For example, priests who are licensed physicians or psychotherapists are also bound by the codes of ethics for those professions, which may bear upon the question of privilege. Priests who serve as school teachers, principals, guidance counselors,

[16] *Buttecali v. United States,* 130 F.2d 172 (1942).
[17] *Id.* at 174.
[18] *Id.*

or directors of foster care homes, shelters for runaways, and day care centers may find their claim of clergy privilege limited (particularly in child abuse reporting contexts) when information comes to them in that role.

With regard to others who serve the Church, only the most limited coverage is available under clergy privilege statutes. Religious men and women (here specifically brothers and sisters) have no special protection because of their profession of vows, but are covered only to the extent of their occupations. Spiritual directors who are not priests have limited coverage. Pastoral associates or parish administrators may have some limited coverage, but it may be effective only when they are working under the direct supervision of a priest. Directors of religious education, youth ministers, catechists, campus ministers, hospital or prison chaplains, and extraordinary ministers of communion are unlikely to have coverage under the privilege statute merely by serving in those roles.

Although most statutes do not define the terms used to determine who is included under the clergy privilege and few courts have occasion to do so, three cases are of some significance in the determination of who is bound under the clergy privilege statutes.

A New Jersey court refused to extend the clergy privilege to a Catholic nun.[19] Sister Margaret Murtha refused to disclose a conversation she had with a young man accused of murder which took place on the night of the alleged incident. She claimed to have had a long-standing counseling relationship with him over a period of five years, beginning when he was one of her students, and had counseled him on family, social, moral, school, and religious problems. The relevant statute prevented disclosure of "a confession or other confidential communication made to [a clergyman] in his professional character, or as a spiritual advisor *in the course of the discipline or practice of the religious body to which he belongs.*"[20] Even though the New Jersey statute had "broadened the privilege to include not only a clergyman or minister but any 'other person or practitioner

[19] *In re Murtha,* 115 N.J. Super. 380, 279 A.2d 889 (1971), *cert. denied,* 59 N.J. 239, 281 A.2d 278 (1971).

[20] N.J. Stat. Ann. sec. 2A:84A-23 (Evidence Rule 29) (emphasis added).

authorized to perform similar functions'[21], the court refused to include Sister Murtha within its scope since it was "unable to find anything in Catholic doctrine or practice that would give (her) the right to claim the priest-penitent privilege."[22] In essence, because the discipline of the Catholic Church did not give Sister Murtha the right to hear confessions, give absolution, or perform other priestly functions, she had no right to preserve the confidentiality of this communication.

The New Jersey decision was distinguished by a federal court in the application of the Missouri statute and federal common law.[23] Sister Dominic Rowe was called to give a deposition but refused to answer questions regarding communications she had with the plaintiff. Sister Rowe maintained that "these communications were made in confidence and under the auspices of her role as plaintiff's spiritual director."[24] She submitted documentation that she had become the plaintiff's spiritual director many years earlier when plaintiff was a postulate seeking admission to her religious order.[25] The court concluded that this relationship was

> sufficient to invoke the priest-penitent privilege under both Missouri and federal law. The sister submitted a number of affidavits to establish that a spiritual director is a recognized office in the Catholic Church, and is considered to be a form of ministry of the Gospel by the Church. It is undertaken by priests and sisters alike. In addition, since Vatican II, the Church has allowed sisters to engage in religious and spiritual direction, in giving retreats and in administering Holy Communion. These are other means by which sisters engage professionally in the ministry of the Gospel . . . (I)n serving as plaintiff's spiritual director, Sister Dominic Rowe occupied such a position within the Church and was performing such a function as to entitle her to the priest-penitent privilege.[26]

[21]*In re Murtha, supra,* at 892.
[22]*Id.* at 893.
[23]*Eckmann v. Board of Education of Hawthorn School District,* 106 F.R.D. 70 (1985).
[24]*Id.* at 71.
[25]*Id.*
[26]*Id.* at 72-3.

It is not clear whether this decision reflects the federal court's perceived differences in the roles Sister Murtha and Sister Rowe had in relation to their communicants or whether the fourteen years between decisions is responsible for a more liberal interpretation of the applicability of the statute. It seems fairly clear, however, that the privilege was granted to Sister Rowe primarily because of her *role* as spiritual director rather than her *state* as a religious woman. There are no other cases dealing with spiritual directors. It is not clear from this case whether a lay person who has formally established a spiritual director's relationship with another can claim the clergy privilege regarding their conversations.

The third case which is relevant in determining who is covered by the privilege statutes dealt with non-ordained draft counsellors working under the supervision of a Presbyterian minister.[27] Reverend Verplank, working as a college chaplain in California at the time of the Vietnam War, was directed by the college to provide draft counseling services to the faculty and students. While he originally undertook to perform this function himself, the rapid increase in the number of people seeking draft counseling forced him to hire a staff for assistance. These counselors were not ordained, but worked under the minister's direct supervision.[28] The court concluded that the activities of the draft counselors

> conform(ed) "at least in a general way" with a significant portion of the activities of a minister of an established Protestant denomination, to the extent necessary to bring them within the privilege covering communications to clergymen.[29]

In addition, the court analogized the relationship between Reverend Verplank and the draft counselors to that between the lawyer and his secretary and paralegals and noted that the attorney privilege has been extended to these nonprofessional representatives.

Again, it is difficult to know how far courts will be willing to extend the holding of *Verplank.* In many areas of the country today, non-ordained persons are filling the roles of pastoral

[27]*In re Verplank,* 329 F. Supp. 433 (1971).
[28]*Id.* at 435-6.
[29]*Id.* at 436.

associate and parish administrator because of the lack of priests to fill these positions. Under the reasoning of *Verplank* an argument can be made that these persons should have the right to claim the clergy privilege; there is no guarantee that this argument will win.

Two phrases used by those states which pattern their privilege statute after the Model Rules of Evidence deserve a brief comment. Some statutes, following the listing of titles defining the clergy, include the terminology "or other similar functionary of a religious organization."[30] Accepted statutory construction would limit these general words as applicable only to those in the same general class as the particular persons enumerated. Although it is possible that this language may provide room for expansion of the privilege to cover persons serving in a variety of ministries, no case has yet defined the scope of these words.

Another phrase which appears in some statutes' definition of the clergy is "an individual reasonably believed so to be by the person consulting him."[31] Again, statutory construction limits these general words to a person "reasonably believed" to be a member of the clergy. Except under the broadest interpretation it is not likely a court would decide that these words include the reasonable belief of the communicant that conversations with a particular person (let us say with a youth minister or pastoral associate) can be kept confidential if that communicant knows the person is not a member of the clergy. However, no court has yet decided the scope of these words.

In summary, based on state statutes and the cases interpreting them, it is rare that a court will extend the clergy privilege to those outside of ordained ministers. Consequently, non-ordained ministers should be fully aware that communications made to them, regardless of the minister's and the communicant's intent, are probably not privileged under civil law.

[30]Alaska, Arkansas, California, Delaware, Hawaii, Maine, Mississippi, Missouri, Nebraska, New Jersey, New Mexico, North Dakota, Oklahoma, South Dakota, Texas, Vermont, Wisconsin.

[31]Alaska, Arkansas, Delaware, Florida, Hawaii, Maine, Nebraska, New Mexico, North Dakota, Oklahoma, South Dakota, Texas, Vermont, Wisconsin.

III. WHAT COMMUNICATIONS ARE COVERED BY THE CLERGY PRIVILEGE?

A. Oral Communications

Although ordained clergy have the broadest coverage under the clergy privilege statutes, not every conversation with a bishop, priest or deacon is privileged. Social pleasantries and other day-to-day conversations between clergy and laity, or among members of the clergy themselves, are not usually made with the required expectation of confidentiality. Casual conversation with a clergyman[32] or conversations concerning business matters[33] or conversations in which the communicant does not seek spiritual advice[34] are not covered by the privilege statutes. In the words of the model statute, in order for the conversation to be privileged, the communication must be made to the clergyman "in his professional character as spiritual advisor."

1. Confession

Sacramental confession is the most uncomplicated of the privileged conversations to discuss. With the exception of West Virginia, every state grants privileged status to communications made in confession and covered by the sacramental seal. Some narrowly drawn and narrowly interpreted statutes, limiting the privilege to communications made in the course of discipline or practice of the religious body,[35] can be analyzed as holding that only these confessional communications are privileged. Obviously, then, only bishops and priests are covered by these narrow privilege statutes since only they can hear sacramental confessions.

The West Virginia privilege statute is unique in that it applies only to actions brought under the divorce and annulment

[32] *Buuck v. Kruckeberg,* 121 Ind. App. 262, 95 N.E.2d 304 (1951, *Burger v. State,* 238 Ga. 171, 231 S.E.2d 769 (1977).

[33] *Nilburn v. Haworth,* 74 Colo. 593, 108 P. 155 (1910), *U.S. v. Gordon,* 493 F. Supp. 822 (N.D.N.Y. 1980), *U.S. v. Dube,* 820 F.2d 886.

[34] *Christensen v. Pestorious,* 189 Minn. 548, 250 N.W. 383 (1933), *State v. Black,* 291 N.W.2d 208 (Minn. 1980).

[35] Arizona, California, Idaho, Indiana, Michigan, Montana, Nevada, Utah, Washington, Wyoming.

statute.[36] However, a strong constitutional argument can be made that the seal of confession set forth in canon law must be respected by civil courts in all proceedings, which will protect the privileged nature of these communications.[37]

2. Spiritual Direction

Distinct from yet closely related to sacramental confession is the practice of spiritual direction.[38] While this ministry is becoming widespread in the Catholic Church today, in the context of privileged communications there is an inability to discuss it with clarity "due to the absence of an authoritative ecclesiastical specification concerning the place of spiritual direction in the general life and ministry of the Church."[39] Just as in the sacrament of reconciliation the penitent confesses to God through the person of the priest, in spiritual direction the primary relationship is that of the one seeking direction and the Lord. In spiritual direction "the real director is the Holy Spirit."[40]

While priests are likely to be the primary ministers of spiritual direction, even

> (i)n the event all priests were able and willing to give direction, the Church would still need others, lay men and women, to share in this ministry.... It is already clear that Catholics not ordained to the priesthood are serving as spiritual directors. It is likely that many more are being called to serve in this ministry.[41]

As one commentator has noted,[42] the confidentiality expected in spiritual direction is very close to that of confession and a critical element in the relationship.

> As an aspect of pastoral ministry, spiritual direction demands of the director practically the same degree

[36]W. Va. Code sec. 48-2-10a (1986 & Supp. 1988).

[37]See text at nn. 68-71 for discussion of constitutional requirements of deferral to a hierarchial church's own law and tribunals.

[38]See generally, Stake, "Professionalism and Confidentiality in the Practice of Spiritual Direction," 43 *The Jurist* 214 (1983).

[39]*Id.* at 214.

[40]*Id.* at 224.

[41]*Id.* at 221.

[42]*Id.* at 224-230.

of trust, silence and discipline that is accepted and imposed upon the priest by the canonical regulation of the seal of confession. In a broader context such confidentiality can be seen as following from the professional responsibility of the director to encourage open dialogue. It can also be viewed from the expectations of the directee that the forum of spiritual direction is a privileged one, that matters revealed–be they penitential in character or not – are done so in the trust that they not be exposed without the directee's explicit prior request.[43]

Some clergy privilege statutes limit communications covered to confessions or admissions of guilt or sin.[44] Since spiritual direction can and does involve a broader discussion than this, confidentiality may not be protected under these statutes. Under the broader statutes, which protect the confidentiality of communications made seeking spiritual advice, comfort, counseling, or guidance,[45] spiritual direction is probably protected.

This broader application of the privilege may, in the end, apply only to ordained spiritual directors, depending on how liberally the statute defines "clergyman," which again leaves open the question of confidentiality and lay spiritual directors. As noted in the *Murtha* and *Eckmann* cases involving religious sisters above,[46] the courts have split in their decisions on whether non-ordained directors ought to be included under the statute.

A constitutional argument, based on free exercise of religion, is difficult to make in this case since canon law does not elaborate on this ministry nor provide guidance (except in limited instances regarding the prohibition on use of information learned in this forum in external decision making[47]) on the scope of confidentiality required. Without a clearer definition of the ministry of spiritual direction in canon law or by the local Ordinary,[48] non-

[43]*Id.* at 225, citations omitted.

[44]*Supra,* n. 35.

[45]Alabama, Colorado, District of Columbia, Florida, Georgia, Kansas, Louisiana, Maryland, Massachusetts, Minnesota, Missouri, New Hampshire, Ohio, Rhode Island, Tennessee, Virginia, West Virginia.

[46]*Supra,* text at nn. 19-26.

[47]Canon 240, §2.

[48]See Stake, *supra* n. 38, 231-322, for a proposed model statute for the ministry of spiritual direction through ecclesiastical legislation.

ordained spiritual directors must assume that the clergy privilege will not cover communications made to them and may wish to advise their directees of this limitation.

3. Pastoral and Marriage Counseling

Prior to society's general acceptance of psychological counseling and therapy, priests have long served as counselors to their parishioners, particularly for marriage-related problems. Even today people often turn first to their pastor before seeking outside help. Correspondingly, clergy and full-time professional ministers often receive some training in psychology and counseling. Sometimes the issues dealt with in pastoral counseling first arise in a confessional or spiritual direction context, yet counseling is clearly distinct from them.

Like spiritual direction, effective counseling can take place only in an atmosphere of trust, respect, and confidentiality. Some states, in recognizing this as an extremely important role for the clergy, have specifically included counseling under their clergy privilege statutes. As noted,[49] others still limit the privilege to confessional contexts. Where these narrow privilege statutes exist, counseling is not protected by the clergy privilege.

A recent case in California illustrates this point.[50] Ms. Edwards, the treasurer of an Episcopal Church parish guild, confessed to the parish's associate pastor that she had embezzled nearly $30,000 of the guild's funds. After receiving absolution for this confession, the associate indicated that she must report this matter to the pastor. Ms. Edwards did so, requesting that their conversation be kept confidential, and told the pastor she had secured a loan to cover the missing funds. The pastor responded that he felt it was his duty to refer the matter to the church wardens, who were responsible for the parish's financial affairs, and asked her to agree to this course of action which she did so. After the wardens sought the advice of the diocesan controller, they felt bound to report the matter to the police.[51]

When the case came to trial, Edwards claimed that her conversation with the pastor was covered by the California clergy

[49]*Supra,* text at n. 35 and n. 44.
[50]*People v. Edwards,* 248 Cal. Rptr. 53 (1988).
[51]*Id.* 54-55.

privilege statute.[52] Upon receiving evidence from the Episcopal bishop on the nature of church law, including the opinion that dual confessions were unusual and that each incident must be treated on a case-by-case basis, the court ruled that only Edwards' confession to the associate was privileged and the conversation with the pastor was "a request for pastoral counselling"[53] not covered by the statute.

Confidentiality in the area of marriage counseling may add an additional complexity if that counseling takes place with both spouses together. Many states recognize the role of the clergy in healing and preserving marriages, and include within the bounds of privilege counseling undertaken with both spouses together.[54] Some states, however, take the strict legal position that for communications to be truly made with the expectation of confidentiality, no third party may be present.[55]

The courts have allowed counseling communications to be protected in one limited way – when the clergyman enters into an agreement with the party or parties that their conversations will be kept confidential. Although California does not include marriage counseling under its privilege statute, one California court did protect the communication between a rabbi and a husband and wife who had sought his help in preserving their marriage.[56] In this case the rabbi had agreed to undertake marriage counseling with the couple "only after an express agreement that their communications to him would be confidential and that neither would call him as a witness in the event of a divorce action."[57] The court found the couple must be held to their bargain and did not require the rabbi's testimony.

In those states where counseling communications are not protected, clergy may wish to think about entering into express agreements with their counselees regarding the matter of con-

[52]Cal. Evid. Code sec. 1030 (West 1966 & Supp. 1988).

[53]*Id.* at 56.

[54]Alaska, Arkansas, Delaware, District of Columbia, Florida, Hawaii, Maine, Nebraska, New Jersey, New Mexico, North Carolina, North Dakota, Oklahoma, Oregon, South Dakota, Texas, Vermont, West Virginia, Wisconsin.

[55]California, Illinois.

[56]*Simrin v. Simrin,* 233 Cal. App. 2d 90, 43 Cal. Rptr. 376 (1965).

[57]*Id.* at 378.

fidentiality. Obviously, this may not be the easiest or most pastoral way of beginning a counseling relationship. On the other hand, both parties need to be aware of the extent to which their conversations are protected by the privilege statute.

With the exception of the draft counseling case,[58] all of the court decisions on matters of pastoral and marriage counseling have involved persons who were clearly members of the clergy. It is difficult to determine how, if at all, the privilege covers non-ordained pastoral counselors, such as those who serve as full-time administrators of parishes and regularly perform these same functions. As already mentioned, non-ordained ministers must be extremely cautious and not assume that the conversations they have with parishioners and counselees are protected by the clergy privilege statute.

Clergy or non-ordained ministers who hold degrees or licenses as therapists are also bound by the standards of their profession and may be protected by privilege statutes which cover mental health practitioners or psychotherapists. As will be discussed below,[59] this may open them to other forms of liability or required testimony.

4. Group Retreat or Renewal Programs

While individual retreats have long been a part of the life of clergy and religious, laity are more frequently taking part in group retreats and renewal programs either at the parish or at retreat houses. Though there are no reported civil cases involving clergy privilege in this context, it is not too difficult to consider circumstances in which questions of confidentiality may arise. Perhaps a hypothetical will suffice.

The Christ Renews His Parish program operates on the parish level with men and women participating separately in small groups. Each group consists of a team (including a priest) who facilitates the program, and participants from whom are drawn the team for the subsequent program. It is made very clear, both during the group retreat and in the team formation period, that all communications made are to be kept solely within the group and are not for general discussion outside of it.

[58]*Supra*, text at n. 27-29.
[59]*Infra*, at section IV, D.

During a team formation session on the subject of reconciliation, one participant, in a heightened state of emotions and with a true sense of seeking forgiveness, confesses to the group that she has been involved in an extra-marital affair and names a prominent parishioner as the co-respondent. Word of this leaks to the man's wife who files a divorce action and later subpoenas all who were present at the group session, including the priest, requiring their testimony regarding the confession.

With one exception, no state will permit this type of communication to remain confidential, but instead will require the testimony of those subpoenaed. The civil law has determined that the presence of third parties removes an essential component of the legal requirement for confidentiality. The New Jersey statute[60] includes in its provisions that a clergyman need not testify to the "confidential relations and communications between and among him and individuals, couples, families or groups with respect to the exercise of his professional counseling role." This is the only statute that includes group counseling within its parameters. Whether or not the hypothetical described above will come under these provisions, and whether or not it will include those group participants other than the priest, is not clear. Consequently, despite the sincere intentions of group retreat and renewal programs to hold sacred the communications made by participants, it should be made clear to all that the legal protection of confidentiality may not extend to these situations.

B. Non-Oral Communications

Probate actions is an area in which the testimony of the clergy may be sought. In fact, probate may be second only to homicide as the issue being litigated in the reported clergy privilege cases. In these instances a priest may be asked to reveal not the content of a communication with a decedent whose will is now being contested, but the competence or state of mind of that person. Courts have held that while the communication between the clergyman and the decedent is protected, the clergyman can be asked to testify to the decendent's mental competence

[60]N.J. Stat. Ann. sec. 2A:84A-23 (West 1976 & Supp. 1988).

without violating the privilege.[61] Iowa, however, has included the observations of a clergyman within the parameters of the privilege.[62]

Logically, this standard would apply to pastoral ministers or extraordinary ministers of communion who visit the sick and are asked to testify to a person's mental competence. Again, these non-ordained ministers are not likely to be able to claim the privilege for the conversations themselves.

In a Massachusetts case the issue arose as to whether or not a clergyman could testify as to what he saw during a conversation with a defendant.[63] Here the trial court allowed a Lutheran minister to testify that while he was traveling in his car with the defendant, the defendant took a handgun from his clothing and placed it in the glove compartment of the car, and that at the end of the trip the defendant had removed the gun and took it with him.[64] In reversing this decision, the appeal court held that the showing of the handgun could be considered a "communication" under the statute, and since both parties admitted that the discussion which took place in the minister's car was in the nature of seeking spiritual advice and therefore privileged, anything the minister saw during the communication was likewise protected.[65] This decision rests on a rather broad interpretation of the statute which does not limit communications to conversations.

While this last incident may stretch the privilege to its outer limits, it provides a glimpse of the extent to which clergy may be called into court for testimony. Again, under narrowly construed statutes, much of this subpoenaed testimony will not fall under the protection of the privilege statutes.

C. *Documents*

As noted above,[66] the fundamental duty to disclose evidence in a legal action applies to documents as well as conversations.

[61] *Snyder v. Poplett*, 98 Ill. App. 3d 359, 424 N.E.2d 396 (1981), *Buuck v. Kruckeberg*, 121 Ind. App. 262, 95 N.E.2d 304 (1951).

[62] *Boyles v. Cora*, 232 Iowa 822, 6 N.W.2d 401 (1942).

[63] *Commonwealth v. Zezima*, 365 Mass. 238, 310 N.E.2d 590 (1974).

[64] *Id.* at 240.

[65] *Id.* at 241.

[66] *Supra*, text at n. 6.

In the strict sense, documents generated by the Church or its clergy and employees are not covered by the clergy privilege. In a very few cases, however, the concept of privilege has been extended to protect some subpoenaed documents from disclosure.

One of the problems inherent in dealing with the confidentiality of documents is the enormous number and kind of records generated by the Church. These include, among others, employment records, social service and adoption records, cemetary records, as well as the documents generated by the matrimonial tribunal. With the exception of the latter, each of these specific kinds of files is likely the subject of individual state statutes regarding the preservation and disclosure of their contents. Without analyzing the laws of every jurisdiction regarding specific kinds of files, it is possible only to make the most generalized comments regarding them, mostly in the nature of general policies on file organization and retention which will be dealt with below.[67]

There is a constitutional argument which can be made to protect certain files from disclosure, namely documents and files specifically regulated by the *Code of Canon Law.* In a long line of cases[68] the United States Supreme Court has held that civil courts should defer to the laws and tribunals of hierarchical religious bodies. Specifically, "the First and Fourteenth Amendments permit hierarchical religious organizations to establish their own rules and regulations for internal discipline and government, and to create tribunals for adjudicating disputes over these matters."[69] Further, "the Constitution requires that civil courts accept (the religious tribunal's) decisions as binding upon them,"[70] "(i)n the absence of fraud, collusion, or arbitrariness."[71] These holdings make canon law an important part of the consideration of confidentiality because the courts are required to accept as privileged matters which the Code expressly makes secret.

[67]*Infra,* text at section V, B, 1.

[68]*Watson v. Jones,* 80 U.S. (13 Wall) 679 (1871); *Gonzalez v. Roman Catholic Archbishop of Manila,* 280 U.S. 1 (1929); *Kedroff v. St. Nicholas Cathedral,* 344 U.S. 94 (1952); *Presbyterian Church v. Hull Church,* 393 U.S. 440 (1969);
Serbian Orthodox Diocese v. Milivojevich, 426 U.S. 696 (1976).

[69]*Serbian Orthodox Diocese v. Milivojevich,* 426 U.S. 696 (1976) at 724.

[70]*Id.* at 725.

[71]*Gonzalez v. Roman Catholic Archbishop of Manila,* 280 U.S. 1 (1929) at 16.

This discussion, then, will be limited to documents or files regulated by canon law, namely, diocesan archives, tribunal files, and clergy personnel files. These are important documents which often attract the attention of people seeking information relevant to litigation. The increase in litigation against dioceses and religious institutions themselves has multiplied the problem.

1. Archives

The *Code of Canon Law* requires specific documents to be kept and protected with the greatest care[72] in three categories: the diocesan archives,[73] the secret archives,[74] and the historical archives.[75] The Code sets forth the kinds of documents to be kept in each and the length of time they are to be held. The chancellor is the primary custodian of these files.[76] In addition, the diocesan bishop is responsible for establishing and preserving parish archives and those of other juridic persons.[77] There are specific canonical requirements regarding each of these archives which establish the retention and removal of documents and limit access to them.[78]

a. Ordinary Archives

Even though the documents in the ordinary archives are presumably not secret (or else they would be in the secret archives), there are restrictions on their use.[79] These restrictions can be interpreted as indicating that there is a degree of confidentiality attributed to these documents. The inspection,[80] removal,[81] or copying[82] of documents in the ordinary archives is strictly controlled. Whether the reason is an administrative concern for the preservation of documents or a concern for the confidentiality

[72]Canon 486, §1.
[73]Canon 486, §2.
[74]Canon 489, §1.
[75]Canon 491, §2.
[76]Canon 482, §1.
[77]Canon 491, §1.
[78]See generally, Dillon, "Confidentiality of Ecclesiastical Records," 30 *Catholic Lawyer* 177 (1986) and Elissa Rinere in this volume.
[79]Canons 487, 488.
[80]Canon 487, §1.
[81]Canon 488.
[82]Canon 487, §2.

of the documents is unclear. There are no norms stated in the canons regarding the retention or destruction of documents kept in the ordinary archives.

b. Historical Archives

Canon law directs the bishop to establish an historical archive "in which documents having historical value are diligently preserved and systematically arranged."[83] There are no specific directives governing this type of archive other than that which gives the bishop the discretion to establish the norms governing the inspection or removal of any document.[84] The Code says nothing about the confidentiality of historical documents.

c. Secret Archives

Canon law requires every diocese to maintain a secret archive.[85] It is to be closed and locked and the documents therein are to be protected most securely.[86] There are some documents specifically designated for storage[87] or normally kept[88] in the secret archives, but the bishop retains the discretion to decide which documents should be put there.[89] In order to avoid dissemination of confidential material, documents may not be removed from the secret archives.[90]

The very fact that there is a secret archive in the diocese would strongly indicate to a civil court that the documents that are in the ordinary and historical archives are not confidential. The diocesan bishop should make it clear if there are any confidential documents in these archives and why they are not kept in

[83]Canon 491, §2.

[84]Canon 491, §3.

[85]Canon 489.

[86]Canon 489, §1.

[87]Documents of criminal cases, canon 489, §2; matrimonial dispensations in the non-sacramental internal forum, canon 1082; register for secret marriages, canon 1133.

[88]Dispensations from impediments and irregularities to orders, canons 1047-1048; decree of dismissal from a religious institute, canon 700; documents relating to the loss of the clerical state by invalidity, penalty or dispensation, canons 290-293. See also, Coriden, Green & Heintschel, eds., *The Code of Canon Law: A Text and Commentary*, New York: Paulist Press, 1985, at 397.

[89]Coriden, Green & Heintschel, *supra* n. 88, at 395.

[90]Canon 489, §1.

the secret archives.

The value of the secret archives in safeguarding truly confidential material may be diminished if all Church documents are designated as part of the secret archives. This is particularly true if files or groups of files are assigned to the secret archives upon indication that the civil court may attempt to subpoena particular documents. In such a case, the court may exercise its exception to the rule of deferral to church law for instances of fraud, collusion, and arbitrariness and waive the application of canonical mandates.

d. Parish Archives

The diocesan bishop is responsible for establishing and preserving the parish archives and for establishing norms regarding the inspection or removal of their documents.[91] The pastor shares in the responsibility to see that the parish registers are accurately inscribed and carefully preserved.[92] According to commentators, "(m)ost of the records are confidential and access to them should be granted only with due care."[93] This statement is not specific enough for a civil court to determine which documents are confidential by church law.

e. Generally

In most cases, the Church will release the public ecclesiastical documents that relate to the canonical status of a person, for example, baptismal, marriage, ordination, religious profession, and death records.[94] There are no reported cases on whether notes appearing on these documents (such as indications in a baptismal record that a person is adopted and the name of the birth parent, or restrictions in the annulment sentence which must be met before remarriage) are also part of the public document or if they are protected by the canon on privacy.[95]

Other documents kept in the various archives which are not expressly made confidential by canon law may be accessible

[91]Canon 491, §1.
[92]Canon 535, §4.
[93]Coriden, Green & Heintschel, *supra* n. 88, at 430.
[94]Dillon, supra n. 78, at 196.
[95]Canon 220.

by civil court process. It is essential, therefore, that *before* a problem arises, the bishop clearly delineates in written form exactly what documents and records are considered to be secret in the eyes of the church. In this way the courts will have a neutral policy from which to determine the documents that are beyond the purview of the court.

When the bishop announces a policy regarding the secrecy of church documents, it should as far as possible be done through his powers of ecclesiastical legislation with reference to the *Code of Canon Law.* The policy should state that it is promulgated under authority of the Code, that the documents are secret by reason of the Code (such as the canonical right to privacy[96]) and that, where applicable, the documents relate solely to the religious status of the individual. Diocesan norms on retention, destruction, and disclosure of documents should be expressly stated by the bishop and it should be noted if the norms differ according to the degree of confidentiality attributed to various documents. While such a policy is never a guarantee that the church's files will be protected from disclosure, it may go a long way in supporting the confidentiality argument.

2. Tribunal Files

There is only one civil statute which specifically protects the information gathered by church tribunals in annulment cases. Louisiana has provided for privileged communications between persons and religious authorities relating to matrimonial rights or status. The statute provides:

> (n)o person shall be required to disclose, by way of testimony or otherwise, or to produce, under subpoena, any privileged communication made to any recognized religious authority in connection with any proceeding or review conducted by said authority relating to the determination or declaration of rights or status of any person regarding any privileged communication....[97]

The statute defines "privileged communications" as

[96]*Id.*

[97]La. Rev. Stat. Ann. sec. 13:3734.2 B (West 1968 & Supp. 1988).

> the acquiring, recording, or transmittal of any information... concerning any facts, opinions, or statements made by any person to any recognized religious authority... for the purpose of obtaining a declaration or decision from the religious authority relative to any person's marital status or rights under the law, doctrine, tenets, or beliefs of a religion... including, but not limited to, any and all records, documentary evidence, transcripts of testimony, opinions, or decisions, correspondence, or memoranda relating thereto.[98]

The statute defines "religious authority" as

> any person or group of persons comprising a tribunal, board, or other type of deliberative body who, under the established laws, doctrine, tenets, or beliefs of that religious body or sect,... is vested with the authority to determine the rights and status of persons subject thereto in matters relating to the validity or nullity of the marriage or persons subject to said laws, doctrine, tenets, or beliefs.[99]

In other jurisdictions of the United States, the protection of tribunal documents and testimony is not so clear.[100] The clergy privilege statute may be of limited help in this case, especially if narrowly written to cover only confessions or if narrowly interpreted by the courts. If the privilege statute does apply, it may be limited to the testimony of the "penitent,"[101] in this case, the petitioner and respondent themselves. Evidence from third parties and expert witnesses may not be covered by strictly construed privilege statutes.[102]

Canon law affords some specific provisions which control the confidentiality of information gathered by the tribunal. One canon

[98] La. Rev. Stat. Ann. sec. 13:3734.2 A (3) (West 1968 & Supp. 1988).

[99] La. Rev. Stat. Ann. sec. 13:3734.2 A (4) (West 1968 & Supp. 1988).

[100] See generally, Dillon, *supra* n. 78; Geary, "Civil Discovery and Confidentiality of Church Documents," Proceedings of the 39th Annual Convention of the Canon Law Society of America, 1977, 82; Serritella, "Confidentiality and the Church," Proceedings of the 23rd National Meeting of Diocesan Attorneys, 1987, 20, at 46-47.

[101] Geary, *supra* n. 100 at 84.

[102] Geary, *supra* n. 100 at 85.

permits the judge to keep evidence confidential and require secrecy if it will harm the reputation of anyone.[103] On the other hand, the Code specifically requires the judge to publish the acts of the case "under pain of nullity," except in cases concerning the public good where "the judge can decree that a given act is not to be shown to anyone, with due concern, however, that the right of defense always remains intact."[104] It is left to the canonical experts to analyze the impact of this canon on the practices of the tribunals. However, civil courts may view the requirement of publication as an indication that complete confidentiality is not required by canon law.

There is only one reported case discussing discovery of tribunal records.[105] A husband sought the testimony of his wife and other witnesses made to the tribunal in the course of annulment proceedings. In characterizing the wife's statements as "penitential"[106] and the tribunal proceedings as required so that the wife "could obtain sanctions from the Catholic Church for separate maintenance and divorce,"[107] the court determined that the clergy privilege statute applied and asserted that "a person must be free to say anything and everything to his Church, at least so long as it is said in a recognized and required proceedings of the religion and to a recognized official of the religion."[108] The court extended the protection of the privilege statute to the testimony of the witnesses since "this collaboration is necessary in a proceeding to obtain sanctions"[109] under the rules of the Catholic Church.

Establishment of a well-drawn tribunal policy guaranteeing the confidentiality of all testimony given in a case may help to protect tribunal files from disclosure. The policy should include the specific canonical requirements of confidentiality in these matters and a statement that the proceedings are strictly religious,

[103]Canon 1455, §3.

[104]Canon 1598, §1.

[105]*Cimijotti v. Paulsen,* 219 F. Supp. 621 (N.D. Iowa 1968), *appeal dismissed,* 323 F.2d 716 (8th Cir. 1963), *on remand,* 230 F. Supp. 39 (N.D. Iowa 1964), *aff'd,* 340 F. 2d 613 (8th Cir. 1965).

[106]*Cimijotti v. Paulsen,* 219 F. Supp. 621 (1963) at 624.

[107]*Cimijotti v. Paulsen,* 230 F. Supp. 39 (1964) at 41.

[108]*Id.*

[109]*Cimijotti v. Paulsen,* 219 F. Supp. at 625.

conducted under the authority of canon law, and affecting only the religious status of the parties. A statement on confidentiality of tribunal proceedings to which all persons participating in those proceedings must agree in writing, and which appears as a clearly marked item on all important tribunal documents, can be useful in defending against a subpoena served by one of the parties.[110] How useful such a written agreement might be in refusing to disclose a file when requested by a non-party litigant has not been addressed.

3. Clergy Personnel Files[111]

While clergy personnel files are not directly mentioned in canon law, the Code does mandate that "(n)o one is permitted to damage unlawfully the good reputation which another person enjoys, nor violate the right of another person to protect his or her own privacy."[112] Though this may be the strongest canonical argument a bishop or religious superior can raise against a subpoena for clergy personnel files, it is not likely to offer a successful defense.

Clergy files may include seminary records, letters of assignment, health records, evaluations, and letters of praise or accusation from parishioners or others with whom the priest has been in contact. In addition, these files may not be located at a single source, but be spread out among the bishop's office, personnel board, vicar for priests office, and the seminary.

There are state laws that govern school records, but seminary files may contain far more than the academic transcript of students, including psychological and formation data. In addition, seminary files may contain information on persons not accepted for ordination by the diocese after completing part of the program of study, those who voluntarily withdrew before ordination, and those who were denied admission to the seminary.

The confidentiality of all these files is in grave doubt. Part of such consideration may be who has access to the files. It is ex-

[110]*Simrin v. Simrin, supra* n. 56, and text regarding enforcement of an express agreement of confidentiality where the privilege statute did not otherwise apply.

[111]See generally Serritella, *supra* n. 100, at 40-46.

[112]Canon 220.

pected that the ordinary and moderator of the curia of the diocese or the superior in a religious order would have universal access. Those in the office generating such files have access to their own documents. The priest or deacon himself may or may not have access to parts of his own file. All others should be excluded from access to these files.

The clergy privilege statute is a weak argument in defense against releasing material from clergy personnel files. Even if the privilege was extended to written communications generally, few, if any, of these documents would fall under the scope of the statutes which require confidential communications to be either "penitential" in character or made "to a clergyman in his role as a spiritual advisor."

In addition, as one commentator has noted,[113]

> courts have not been sympathetic to the First Amendment free exercise arguments made supporting the confidentiality of communications which have not otherwise come under the clergy-penitent privilege. In upholding a *subpoena duces tecum* for a priest's personnel file, the court held that the production of these documents would 'not interfere with the Bishop's right to believe as he chooses and to engage in religious observances of his faith... Information in the possession of the church has always been subject to civil process. This is precisely why states have adopted statutes creating a priest-penitent privilege. If the Bishop were right about the protection afforded by the (free exercise clause of the) Constitution, there would be no need for the privilege.'[114]

There are two cases which have considered the confidentiality of clergy personnel files. In Delaware a priest sued law enforcement officials for alleged damage to his reputation resulting from false accusations of criminal activity.[115] The defendants subpoenaed the priest's personnel files from his bishop seeking evidence on his reputation. The court held that those documents "pertaining to his performance as a priest clearly come within

[113]Serritella, *supra* n. 100, 45-46.
[114]*Id*, citing *Pagano v. Hadley*, 100 F.R.D. 758 (D.C.Del. 1984).
[115]*Pagano v. Hadley*, 100 F.R.D. 758 (D.C.Del. 1984).

the scope of permissible discovery"[116] and could not be withheld by the diocese. The court found it could not sustain the bishop's position that the files come within the clergy-penitent privilege since it was unlikely that many of the documents were communications from the priest to his bishop (in his role as the priest's spiritual advisor)[117] though it exempted from discovery those documents in this limited category.

In an unpublished case from Arizona,[118] a pastor sued his parishioners for libel. The defendants raised the affirmative defense of truth and were granted an order allowing discovery of his diocesan personnel records to substantiate this defense. Although the diocese argued that revelation of church records would violate the First Amendment, the court ruled that the priest had opened himself to the inquiry when he initiated the litigation.[119]

An argument supporting the confidentiality of clergy personnel files would be strengthened by reliance on clearly stated canon law, but the canon on privacy may not provide a civil court with the mandate it needs. In addition, litigants may be able to surface canon law experts on both sides of the issue, putting the civil court in a position where it cannot constitutionally decide which expert is correct.[120] If the court cannot determine that church law exists on a question before it, the court need not defer to that law.

Finally, in the current litigious society in which dioceses and religious orders have been threatened with liability for actions of priests and others about whom they had prior knowledge of psychological problems, it is not unlikely that information about even those persons not incardinated in a diocese will be sought by an aggressive attorney. This may be particularly true if the seminary provided references on a former student to a subsequent school or employer. Two issues must be raised on this issue. First, when does providing accurate references on a person cross the line into the area of defamation? Second, at what point has

[116]*Id.* at 760.

[117]*Id.*

[118]*Curry v. Even.* See Ball, "Current Litigation," 29 *Catholic Lawyer* 207 (1984) at 215.

[119]*Id.*

[120]Serritella, *Proceedings Nineteenth National Meeting of Diocesan Attorneys,* 107, April, 1983, at 122.

a person paid his debt or sufficiently received help for a problem that referral to it does a severe injustice to him? These, perhaps, are matters that must be carefully discussed with diocesan and religious order officials and their legal counsel.

IV. LIMITATIONS ON THE PRIVILEGE

A. The Effects of Waiver

While the preceding sections of this article set forth the extent to which confidential communications made to clergy and other non-ordained ministers may be covered by the clergy privilege statutes, that entire analysis may be rendered invalid by the concept of waiver. In 28 states,[121] ownership of the privilege is placed primarily in the hands of the penitent or communicant. In these jurisdictions, if the communicant waives the privilege (asking the clergyman to testify to the nature and content of their conversation) the clergyman may have no right to claim the privilege on his own behalf. Likewise, if the communicant is deceased or missing, the clergyman may have no right to claim the privilege on behalf of the communicant. In one case, a Massachusetts court held that when the communicant waives the privilege, the clergyman must testify and may be held in contempt of court if he does not.[122]

Clearly, the ability of the communicant to waive the protection of the privilege forcing the clergy to testify creates a direct conflict with the seal of confession commanded by canon law which declares that the priest himself must protect the secrecy of the confessional. Though no reported case has raised the constitutional argument of deferral to church law, that is the strongest defense to such a move by the communicant.

Since canon law protects no communications outside of sacramental confession, the church law argument cannot be used in many instances in which waiver by the communicant may be invoked. Two examples may give some idea how waiver (or non-waiver) of the privilege by the communicant can affect the

[121]Arizona, Arkansas, Connecticut, Idaho, Iowa, Kentucky, Louisiana, Massachusetts, Minnesota, Mississippi, Montana, Nevada, New York, North Carolina, North Dakota, Oklahoma, Oregon, Pennsylvania, Rhode Island, South Carolina, South Dakota, Tennessee, Texas, Utah, Vermont, Washington, West Virginia, Wisconsin.

[122]*Commonwealth v. Kane,* 388 Mass. 128, 445 N.E.2d 598 (1983).

outcome of a legal matter.

In the first instance,[123] an unscrupulous person may seek counseling from a number of different clergymen, admitting to each of them different facts regarding an incident in which he was involved. When brought to trial, this person can waive the privilege (and compel testimony) from the clergyman to whom he has "confessed" facts most favorable to his defense, at the same time not waiving the privilege with regard to conversations with the other clergy (preventing their testimony) to whom he has given different stories.

In the second instance, a couple participating in joint marriage counseling with a clergyman may nonetheless end up in a divorce action. If in attempting to reconcile the spouses the clergyman has encouraged open and honest admissions of failure on their parts, the spouse feeling most wronged may seek to waive the privilege and compel the testimony of the clergyman as to the other party's failings.

Placing the ownership of the privilege in the clergy as well as the communicant is obviously to the benefit of the clergy. In addition, it may protect a communicant being pressured to waive the privilege from doing so, since the clergyman can claim it on his own behalf and refuse to testify. Finally, it may strengthen the confidence of members of all religious communities to make such confidences to their clergy and seek forgiveness if they know that these communications will be protected from revelation to outside sources.

B. When Can the Privilege Be Claimed?

The clergy privilege exists as an exception to the rule that all are required to give evidence. This generally is understood to mean that the privilege can be claimed in court proceedings where the state's rules of evidence apply.

Trial court proceedings are not the only forum in which a clergyman may be asked to testify. Subpoenas may be issued for evidence by grand juries, administrative agencies, or legislative committees. State statutes which do not give protection to confidential communications in all civil fora may leave the clergyman

[123] Reese, "Confidential Communications to the Clergy," 24 *Ohio State Law Journal* 55 (1963) at 85.

and the communicant open to demands for testimony in settings just as damaging to needs for confidentiality as in trial courts.

C. Duty to Warn

One of the fundamental considerations used to support the clergy privilege as an exception to the general rules of evidence is that the injury to the relationship of the clergy and communicant caused by the disclosure of the informatin would be greater than the benefit gained by bringing all evidence into the light. Courts have struggled with the balancing required by this formulation when the communication shared with the clergyman (or another professional covered by a similar privilege) indicates that the communicant may cause a serious injury to himself or another. In these instances the court may demand that the privilege give way to a "duty to warn."

The leading case in this area involved a psychologist whose patient confided to him the intention to kill his former girl friend.[124] Although the campus police were notified, neither the girl nor her parents knew of the threat. The court found that

> (w)hen a therapist determines, or pursuant to the standards of his profession should determine, that his patient presents a serious danger of violence to another, he incurs an obligation to use reasonable care to protect the intended victim against such danger . . . (I)t may call for him to warn the intended victim or others likely to apprise the victim of the danger, to notify the police, or to take whatever other steps are reasonably necessary under the circumstances.[125]

The rationale of the *Tarasoff* case was the basis for the parents of a suicide victim bringing a lawsuit against the clergy and other non-ordained counselors of a church in the widely-reported case *Nally v. Grace Community Church of the Valley.*[126] Although this case was originally labeled one of clergy malpractice, a con-

[124]*Tarasoff v. Regents of the University of California,* 17 Cal.3d 425, 131 Cal. Rptr. 14, 551 P.2d 334 (1976).

[125]*Id.* at 20.

[126]47 Cal. 3d 278, 253 Cal. Rptr. 97, 763 P.2d 948 (Nov. 23, 1988).

cept of dubious legal soundness,[127] the California Court of Appeals[128] characterized the allegations as a negligent failure to prevent suicide and requiring the court to "impose a duty of due care on those who undertake a counseling relationship with mentally disturbed suicidal individuals, whether those counselors are affiliated with a religious institution or not."[129]

Most recently the California Supreme Court reversed this decision and held that pastoral, non-therapist counselors had no duty to refer potentially suicidal persons to a professional therapist and thus could not be held liable for negligence following that person's suicide. The majority opinion reasoned

> (e)ven assuming that workable standards of care could be established in the present case, an additional difficulty arises in attempting to identify with precision those to whom the duty should apply. Because of the differing theological views espoused by the myriad of religions in our state and practiced by church members, it would certainly be impractical, and quite possibly unconstitutional, to impose a duty of case on pastoral counselors. Such a duty would necessarily be intertwined with the religious philosophy of the particular denomination or ecclesiastical teachers of the religious entity.[130]

It appears that limitations on the clergy privilege through a required "duty to warn" about information received from a communicant regarding foreseeable harm to himself or others will not be imposed by the courts at this time. However, when the stakes are raised in public policy matters, limitations on the privilege are readily agreed to by the legislatures and may be imposed by the courts.

[127]See generally, Paprocki, "Malpractice in the Ministry," 3 *The Compleat Lawyer* 18 (1986); Ericsson, "Clergy Malpractice: Ramifications of a New Theory," 16 *Valparaiso University Law Review* 163 (1981); Milne, " 'Bless me Father, for I am about to sin . . .': Should Clergy Counselors Have a Duty to Protect Third Parties," 22 *Tulsa Law Journal* 139 (1968); Note, "Made Out of Whole Cloth? A Constitutional Analysis of the Clergy Malpractice Concept," 19 *California Western Law Review* 507 (1983); Ericsson, *Clergy Malpractice: An Illegal Legal Theory*, Merrifield, VA: The Center for Law and Religious Freedom, 1986.

[128]*Nally v. Grace Community Church of the Valley*, 240 Cal. Rptr. 215 (1987).

[129]*Id.* at 219.

[130]*Nally v. Grace Community Church of the Valley*, 253 Cal. Rptr. 97 (1988) at 109.

D. Mandatory Child Abuse Reporting Acts

Analysis of the state statutes on privileged communications indicate that the exception to the general grants of privilege most often made by the legislatures is in the area of child abuse reporting and requiring testimony at subsequent hearings or trials on these cases. The public has a heightened awareness of the destruction caused by child abuse and has become increasingly willing to limit testimonial privileges in order to bring the perpetrators of child abuse and neglect to justice.

Clergy are not the only professionals whose privilege not to disclose information has been restricted in these cases. Physicians, nurses, psychologists, and many others who normally do not have to testify respecting conversations and admissions made by their patients or clients have lost the right to refuse disclosure of this information. Though clergy retain their privilege in some states, child abuse and neglect statutes are amended each year and the ability of authorities to uncover these crimes is consistently being strengthened.

At the present time, sixteen states[131] have abrogated the clergy privilege for testimony in matters of child abuse. Seventeen states[132] have included clergy among those required to report suspected child abuse or neglect to the authorities. It is not clear from the statutes whether mandatory reporting requirements will require testimony from the clergy in subsequent hearings on these matters. Some states which have made clergy mandatory reporters, retain the privilege for some or all communications made to clergy. There are no reported cases on this somewhat confusing situation.

Though litigation on this point has been infrequent, one case created a sensation in the media. In Florida, a minister who refused to divulge the confidential communications made to him by a parishioner charged with sexual abuse of a young girl was held

[131] Alabama, Arkansas, Delaware, Idaho, Iowa, Maryland, Michigan, Missouri, Nevada, New Hampshire, New Mexico, North Dakota, Oklahoma, Rhode Island, Texas, West Virginia.

[132] Connecticut, Mississippi, Minnesota, Nebraska, Nevada, New Hampshire, New Jersey, New Mexico, North Carolina, Oklahoma, Oregon, Pennsylvania, Rhode Island, Tennessee, Texas, Utah, Wyoming.

in contempt of court and sentenced to sixty days in jail.[133] The conviction was vacated when the Florida legislature responded to the public outcry and restored the clergy privilege of not disclosing penitential communications to the child abuse laws.

One person who seems immune from the public outcry in this area is the Texas Attorney General who ruled that a minister is responsible for reporting a case of child abuse, even when that information was confidentially disclosed to him by a parishioner, and is required to testify in a child abuse proceeding.[134] Since no exceptions were created under the statute, which requires any person with knowledge to make such reports, he determined that the Texas law does not excuse the clergy from a duty to report.

The abrogation of the clergy privilege in matters of child abuse reporting collides with the canonical requirements of the seal of confession. As can be expected, many priests have indicated their determination to be held in contempt of court rather than reveal these confidences.

While abrogating the clergy privilege for child abuse matters, Utah has excepted from this abrogation communications received in sacramental confession.[135] However, this statute still requires that

> if a clergyman or priest receives information about abuse or neglect from any source other than the confession of the perpetrator, he is required to give notification on the basis of that information even though he may have also received a report of abuse or neglect from the confession of the perpetrator. Exemption of notification requirements for a clergyman or priest does not exempt a clergyman or priest from any other efforts required by law to prevent further abuse or neglect by the perpetrator.[135]

An additional concern to clergy in the area of required child abuse reporting arises for those who serve in other roles, such

[133] *Mellish v. Florida*, No. 84-1930 (Fla. Ct. App., 4th Dist., filed Sept. 4, 1984). See 4 *Religious Freedom Reporter* 313, November 1984; Duin, "Judge Dismisses a Case Against Pastor Who Refused to Break a Confidence," 29 *Christianity Today* 48 (Sept. 6, 1985).

[134] Op. Tex. Att'y Gen. No. JM-342 (1985).

[135] Utah Code Ann. sec. 62A-4-503(3) (1986 & Supp. 1968).

as physicians, teachers, mental health professionals, guidance counselors, social workers, and administrators of foster care or day care facilities. This last group may even include pastors whose parishes sponsor day care services on parish property.[136] These professionals, among others, can be mandatory reporters of child abuse. There is no reported litigation on whether or not, for example, a priest who teaches high school is a required reporter if information regarding child abuse comes to him in his role as a teacher rather than as a priest. It may never be clear whether the student who approaches a priest-teacher to disclose such abuse has perhaps chosen to speak to this particular teacher because he happens to be a priest. Likewise, a priest who is degreed and licensed as a psychologist may face a dilemma in whether information on child abuse is coming to him in his pastoral or therapeutic role.

It should be noted that three states have created mandatory reporting requirements for abuse to the elderly and handicapped. The clergy privilege has been retained for these matters in Arizona and Nebraska, but abrogated in Minnesota.[137]

Giving all due regard to the canonical requirements of confidentiality, it is the best interests of dioceses and religious orders to develop guidelines and standards for clergy and non-ordained ministers regarding how they should respond when information of child abuse or neglect comes to them. Not every piece of information can be protected from disclosure by canon law or civil law rules of privilege. As a matter of justice to the children, the Church, above all others, should see that they are protected.

V. SUGGESTIONS FOR IMPROVING THE PROTECTION OF CONFIDENTIALITY IN CIVIL LAW

A. Clergy Privilege Statutes

Based on the discussion above, it is apparent that some clergy privilege statutes can be significantly improved. Before undertaking any of these particular measures, however, two cautions are in order. First, attempts to change the statute should be undertaken on a state-wide, interfaith basis. This will require

[136] *Forest Hills Early Learning Center, Inc. v. Lukhard,* 661 F. Supp. 300 (E.D. Va. 1987).
[137] Arizona, Nebraska, Washington.

careful wording of the amendments to include all faith traditions equally under this coverage. It also will insure a broad-based coalition in support of the changes. Second, it may be wise to lobby the legislature for the broadest statement of the privilege covering all individuals who work for religious bodies and all of the ministries in which they engage. Since the privilege exists as an exception to a general rule, reaching for too much is bound to fail.

Changes that should be attempted include the following matters. First, the statute should insure that the clergyman, as well as the communicant, holds the privilege and that waiver by the communicant does not force the clergyman to testify.

Second, the clergy should be able to claim the privilege in all cases, proceedings and hearings under the auspices of the civil government. Particularly, the West Virginia statute which limits claims of privilege to divorce actions is ripe for amendment. In the area of child abuse, litigation is likely the last step in the process. Testimony is often demanded in administrative hearings which determine placement of the child during further proceedings. If the privilege is going to be effectively claimed, it must be available at such hearings.

Third, in order to at least protect the canonical mandates of confessional secrecy, abrogations of the clergy privilege in child abuse and neglect matters should be eliminated, at the very least in regard to communications received in the confessional. It is not clear given society's strong abhorrence of child abuse whether abrogations of the clergy privilege can be completely eliminated. The Church should also place a high priority on the health and safety of children. Clear guidelines should be promulgated to all who work in ministry regarding circumstances in which allegations of child abuse should be reported.

B. *Internal Policies*

There are policies for dioceses and religious orders which can help protect the confidentiality of information in the possession of the Church or one of its ministers. Some of these policies can be strengthened if they are promulgated under the authority of the *Code of Canon Law* by particular ecclesiastical legislation and designed so appeal and final judgment of the policy rests with the tribunal.

The most important concept in designing policies concerning confidentiality is that the policies are clear and consistently implemented. That requires, first, that the policy be widely disseminated and clearly explained to all those who may need to know its contents. Second, and most important, it is imperative that the policy be adhered to strictly. If a diocesan policy limits access to church files, but the church does not diligently enforce that policy, a court may determine the policy to be a sham and disregard pleas for confidentiality.

1. File Policies

Policies regarding files and documents should include among their provisions indications of who has access to files, strict limitations on access to particular files, what should properly be kept in the file, and how long the file should be kept. The policy may also state whether there is any appeal for a denial of access and with whom the final determination rests.

An important consideration regarding what is to be kept in clergy personnel files concerns letters of complaint or accusation against a priest. These letters should be kept in the priest's file attaching to them a memorandum of what action was taken to deal with the accusation. Such action might include, though is not limited to, memoranda of discussions of the charge with the priest, reports that the charge was determined to be unfounded, or referrals of the priest to professional counseling. A file containing accusations against a priest, even if unsubstantiated, will indicate to civil authorities that the diocese has been put on notice as to the priest's behavior and this may result in punitive damages against the diocese if the priest's guilt is proved.

One important factor must be kept in mind regarding the destruction of documents and files. Courts have found criminal violations of obstruction of justice statutes where a party has destroyed documents.[138] Under these statutes, an individual violates the statute if, while a case is pending or while a grand jury is impanelled, or after being informed of agency or congressional action, he or she destroys documents. Another statute[139]

[138] 18 U.S.C. sec. 1503, 1505.
[139] 18 U.S.C. sec. 1512.

makes it a crime to destroy documents prior to the commencement of an official proceeding. An individual destroying documents under these circumstances may be guilty of a criminal violation as well as facing a contempt citation.

As noted above, Church officials should consider formulating clear guidelines covering the circumstances under which and procedures for reporting suspected cases of child abuse. As appropriate, there may also be policies on the duty to warn of other serious acts, such as possible suicides or threats against the life of another.

There should be a well-defined system for routing requests for information–especially subpoenas–so that they reach the right hands as soon as possible. Subpoenas can be presented at any diocesan location and each should know the procedure to follow when such documents are received. If there are delays in getting them to the diocesan or religious order official who is charged with seeking legal advice, an attorney may have fewer options in dealing with the requests effectively.

2. Policies Regarding Non-ordained Ministers

Following the guidelines set forth by one court determining who qualified as a minister under certain statutes,[140] dioceses may wish to consider policies which clarify the relationship of non-ordained ministers. Such policies should include for each position to be covered the requirements of a set course of study, a certification process upon completion of studies, assignment to a specific ministry or parish and the direction that they work under the supervision of a priest. No pastor should be allowed to grant the title of a position covered by this policy to anyone who has not met the requirements. This policy may not bring non-ordained ministers within the scope of privilege statutes and part of the certification process should include a clear explanation to these ministers of the limitations on their claims of confidentiality with an encouragement that they make these limits known to those with whom they work.

A caveat to this type of policy is the concern for ascending liability. The closer the relationship of individuals who work for the

[140]*Supra*, n. 16.

Church and the institution, the more likely it is that the institution will be held accountable for their actions. Church officials may want to carefully weigh these concerns in the balance.

C. *Relationship Between Canonical and Civil Law Experts*

As was stated at the beginning of this article, the best statutory analysis cannot serve as a substitute for direct legal advice. Church officials should not hesitate to seek help from their legal counsel in the earliest stages of planning and drafting policies to protect the confidentiality of Church communications. The cost of planning and advice is far less than the cost of litigation.

After examining the civil law rules of confidentiality and privileged communications, Church officials may want to designate local canon law experts (chancellor, officialis, and others) to discuss with legal counsel their concerns regarding the limitations of the local statute. That discussion can most effectively take place with all canonical and legal experts on a state-wide basis, perhaps in a meeting convened by the local Catholic Conference where that body exists. Canon law experts should not hesitate to express their concerns regarding the impact of the civil law on effective ministry. Attorneys and lobbyists should be clear on how much can be expected from the state legislature.

Officials of religious orders have special problems, particularly where the province extends across state lines. Because of the peculiarities of individual states, it is wise to seek local legal counsel in each state where members are assigned or property is held. In addition, religious orders may consider the possibility of creating a body similar to that of the Diocesan Attorneys Association in which the legal counsels of religious orders can discuss items of mutual concern.

VI. CONCLUSION

Protecting the confidentiality of religious communications and church documents from civil process is a difficult assignment and there are no guarantees that any one strategy will work. This process requires a knowledgeable and effective team which can translate the mandates of canon law into understandable guidelines for ministers and policies compatible with the laws of the government. With what is at stake in many cases, however, motivation should be high to make the assignment a success.

CONFIDENTIALITY AND MALPRACTICE BIBLIOGRAPHY

Legal Periodicals

Barker, Edward, "Clergy Negligence: Are Juries Ready to Sit in Judgment?," 22 *Trial* 56-59 (July, 1986).

Bergman, Ben Zion, "Is the Cloth Unraveling? A First Look at Clergy Malpractice," 9 *San Fernando Valley Law Review* 47-66 (1981).

Breecher, Maury M., "Ministerial Malpractice: Is It a Reasonable Fear?," 16 *Trial* 11-14 (July, 1980).

Callahan, Michael Janes, "Historical Inquiry Into the Priest-Penitent Privilege," 36 *The Jurist* 328-337 (1976).

Cole, William A., "Religious Confidentiality and the Reporting of Child Abuse: A Statutory and Constitutional Analysis," 21 *Columbia Journal of Law and Social Problems* 1-51 (1987).

Coleman, Phyllis, "'Shrinking' the Clergyperson Exemption to Florida's Mandatory Child Abuse Reporting Statute," 12 *Nova Law Review* 115-145 (1987).

Dillon, Edward J., "Confidentiality of Ecclesiastical Records," 30 *Catholic Lawyer* 177-197 (1986).

Ericsson, Samuel E., "Clergyman Malpractice: Ramifications of a New Theory," 16 *Valparaiso University Law Review* 163-184 (1981).

Griffith, Ezra E.H. and Young, John L., "Pastoral Counseling and the Concept of Malpractice," 15 *Bulletin of the American Academy of Psychiatry and the Law* 257 (1987).

Hogan, Edward A. Jr., "A Modern Problem on the Privilege of the Confessional," 6 *Loyola Law Review* 1-14 (1951).

Kuhlmann, Fred L., "Communications to Clergymen–When Are They Privileged?," 2 *Valparaiso University Law Review* 265-295 (1968).

Little, Sarah Morgan, "Counsel by Clergy: Is it Privileged?," 10 *Family Advocate* 24 (1987).

Milne, Terry Wuester, "'Bless me Father, for I am about to sin . . .': Should Clergy Counselors Have a Duty to Protect Third Parties," 22 *Tulsa Law Journal* 139-165 (1986).

Mitchell, Mary Harter, "Must Clergy Tell? Child Abuse Reporting Requirements Versus the Clergy Privilege and Free Exercise of Religion," 71 *Minnesota Law Review* 723-825 (1987).

Note, "Catholic Sisters, Irregularly Ordained Women and the Clergy-Penitent Privilege," 9 *University of California, Davis*

Law Review 523-547 (1976).
Note, "Clergy Malpractice: Should Pennsylvania Recognize a Cause of Action for Improper Counseling by a Clergyman?" 92 *Dickinson Law Review* 223-251 (1987).
Note, "Clergy Malpractice: Making Clergy Accountable to a Lower Power," 14 *Pepperdine Law Review* 137-161 (1986).
Note, "Clergy Malpractice: Taking Spiritual Counseling Conflicts Beyond Intentional Tort Analysis," 19 *Rutgers Law Journal* 419-450 (1988).
Note, "Church Tort Liability in Spite of First Amendment Protection," 12 *Southern University Law Review* 37-46 (1985).
Note, "Evidence: 'Is There a Time to Keep Silence?'–The Priest-Penitent Privilege in Oklahoma," 27 *Oklahoma Law Review* 258-264 (1974).
Note, "Intentional Infliction of Emotional Distress by Spiritual Counsellors: Can Outrageous Conduct by 'Free Exercise'?," 84 *Michigan Law Review* 1296-1325 (1986).
Note, "Made Out of Whole Cloth? A Constitutional Analysis of the Clergy Malpractice Concept," 19 *California Western Law Review* 507-544 (1983).
Note, "Privileged Communications to Clergymen," 1 *Catholic Lawyer* 199-213 (1955).
Note, "Privileged Communications–Clergyman-Communicant Privilege–Application to Clergyman Directed Draft Counseling," 18 *Wayne Law Review* 883-900 (1972).
Note, "Religious Counseling–Parents Allowed to Pursue Suit Against Church and Clergy for Son's Suicide–Nally v. Grace Community Church," 1985 *Arizona State Law Journal* 213-236 (1985).
Note, "Seeing in a Mirror Dimly? Clergy Malpractice as a Cause of Action: Nally v. Grace Community Church," 15 *Capital University Law Review* 349-369 (1986).
Note, "Striking Down the Clergyman-Communicant Privilege Statutes: Let Free Exercise of Religion Govern," 62 *Indiana Law Journal* 397-423 (1987).
Note, "Texas' Clergyman-Penitent Privilege and the Duty to Report Suspected Child Abuse," 38 *Baylor Law Review* 231-248 (1986).
Note, "The Clergy-Communicant Privilege: Blessed Are the Meek, For They Shall Remain Silent," 65 *North Carolina Law Review* 1390-1408 (1987).

Note, "The Clergy-Penitent Privilege and the Child Abuse Reporting Statute: Is the Secret Sacred?," 19 *John Marshall Law Review* 1031-1051 (1986).

Note, "When must a Priest Report Under a Child Abuse Reporting Statute?–Resolution to the Priests' Conflicting Duties," 21 *Valparaiso University Law Review* 431-465 (1987).

Paprocki, Thomas J., "Malpractice in the Ministry," 3 *The Compleat Lawyer* 18-20 (1986).

Reese, Seward, "Confidential Communications to the Clergy," 24 *Ohio State Law Journal* 55-88 (1963).

Regan and Macartney, "Professional Secrecy and Privileged Communications," 2 *The Catholic Lawyer* 3-14 (1956).

Silas, Faye A., "Embattled Clergy," 72 *ABA Journal* 36 (February 1986).

Smith, Michael Clay, "The Pastor on the Witness Stand: Toward a Religious Privilege in the Courts," 29 *Catholic Lawyer* 1-21 (1984).

Stake, Ronald P., "Professionalism and Confidentiality in the Practice of Spiritual Direction," 43 *The Jurist* 214-232 (1983).

Stoyles, Robert L., "The Dilemma of the Constitutionality of the Priest-Penitent Privilege–The Application of the Religion Clauses," 29 *University of Pittsburgh Law Review* 27-63 (1967).

Wise, Helen Sunny, "Clergy Malpractice/First Amendment Under Siege," 8 *Los Angeles Lawyer* 20-21 (1985).

Yellin, Jacob M., "The History and Current Status of the Clergy-Penitent Privilege," 23 *Santa Clara Law Review* 95-156 (1983).

Legal Periodicals—Related Topics

Esbeck, Carl H., "Tort Claims Against Churches and Ecclesiastical Officers: The First Amendment Considerations," 89 *West Virginia Law Review* 1-114 (1986).

Note, "A Suggested Privilege for Confidential Communications with Marriage Counsellors," 106 *University of Pennsylvania Law Review* 266-278 (1957).

Note, "Duty to Warn Versus Duty to Maintain Confidentiality: Conflicting Demands on Mental Health Professionals," 20 *Suffolk University Law Review* 579-615 (1986).

Note, "The Psychiatric Duty to Warn: Walking a Tightrope of Uncertainty," 56 *University of Cincinnati Law Review* 269-293 (1987).

Note, "The Psychotherapist-Client Testimonial Privilege: Defining the Professional Involved," 34 *Emory Law Journal* 777-826 (1985).

Ungar, L., "Privilege and the Marriage Counsellor," 5 *Brooklyn Bar* 49-55 (1953).

Other Periodicals

Casey, Rick, "Pastor Jailed; Pastoral Confidence Issue," 17 *National Catholic Reporter* 24 (May 29, 1981).

Duin, Julia, "A Pastor Faces Legal Action for Refusing to Break Confidence," 28 *Christianity Today* 80 (October 5, 1984).

Duin, Julia, "Judge Dismisses a Case Against Pastor Who Refused to Break a Confidence," 29 *Christianity Today* 48 (September 6, 1985).

Fortune, Marie M., "Confidentiality and Mandatory Reporting: A False Dilemma," 103 *The Christian Century* 582-583 (June 18-25, 1986).

Fox, Martin, "Minister Ordered to Disclose Couple's Confidential Talks: Parties Waive Privilege in Divorce Case," 194 *New York Law Journal* 1 (November 14, 1985).

Gallet, Jeffrey H., "The Confidentiality Privilege for Members of the Clergy," 194 *New York Law Journal* 1 (November 22, 1985).

Geary, Patrick F., "Civil Discovery and Confidentiality of Church Documents," *CLSA Proceedings* 39 (1977), 82-86.

Goldman, Ari L., "Three Cases Challenged Privacy of Talks with Clergy," 131 *Chicago Daily Law Bulletin* 3 (August 28, 1985).

Hammett, R. and Sofield, L., "Some Reflections on Confidentiality," 51 *Sisters* 150-152 (November, 1979).

Holzberg, Bryan, "Minister Must Testify in Divorce Hearing," 8 *National Law Journal* 3 (December 9, 1985).

McMenamin, Robert W., "Clergy Malpractice," 90 *Case & Comment* 3-6 (September/October, 1985).

Menendez, "Clergy Confidential: Confession May be Good for the Soul, But It's a Problem for the State," 39 *Church and State* 128 (1986).

Ostling, Richard N., "Confidence and the Clergy," 124 *Time* 66 (October 1, 1984).

Ranii, David, "Piercing the Veil of the Confessional: Damages Sought from Diocese: Did Bishop Have a Duty to Act?," 5 *National Law Journal* 3 (May 16, 1983).

Reifsnyder, Richard W., "Who Decides What is Confidential?," 103 *The Christian Century* 1109-1110 (December 10, 1986).
Sarno, Gregory G., "Pastoral Malpractice: A Wolf in Sheep's Clothing?," 83 *Liberty* 5-7 (March/April, 1988).
Scott, Jeffrey Warren, "Confidentiality and Child Abuse: Church and State Collide," 103 *The Christian Century* 174-175 (February 19, 1986).
Scott, Jeffrey Warren, "Why Clergy Shouldn't Tell," 81 *Liberty* 14-15 (September/October, 1986).
Serritella, James A., "Confidentiality, the Church and the Clergy," *CLSA Proceedings* 48 (1986), 83-93.
Smith, W., "Some Problems of Confidentiality and How They May Be Avoided," 41 *Linacre* 212-216 (August, 1974).
Thomsen, Marilyn, "Clergy Malpractice Goes to Court–Is Religious Freedom on the Line?," 80 *Liberty* 13-17 (November/December, 1985).

Books

Annotation, "Matters to Which the Privilege Covering Communication to Clergyman or Spiritual Advisor Extends," 71 A.L.R.3d 794-838.
Annotation, "Who is 'Clergyman' or the Like Entitled to Assert Privilege Attaching to Communications to Clergymen or Spiritual Advisors," 49 A.L.R.3d 1205-1213.
Ericsson, Samuel E., *Clergy Malpractice: Constitutional and Political Issues* Oak Park, IL: The Center for Law and Religious Freedom, 1981.
Ericsson, Samuel E., *Clergy Malpractice: An Illegal Legal Theory* Merrifield, VA: The Center for Law and Religious Freedom, 1986.
Gumper, Lindell L., *Legal Issues in the Practice of the Ministry* Birmingham, MI: Psychological Studies, 1981.
Malony, H. Newton, Needham, Thomas L. and Southard, Samuel, *Clergy Malpractice* Philadelphia: The Westminster Press, 1986.
McMenamin, Robert W., *Clergy Malpractice* Buffalo, N.Y.: William S. Hein & Co., Inc., 1986.
McMenamin, Robert W. and Kralovec, William P., *Clergy & Teacher Malpractice: Recognition and Prevention* Portland: Jomac Publishing, Inc., 1987.
Plantamura, Michael G., "The Clergyman-Penitent Privilege," in

Testimonial Privileges (Stone and Liebman, eds.) Colorado Springs: Shepard's/McGraw-Hill, 1983.
Tiemann, William Harold and Bush, John C., *The Right to Silence: Privileged Clergy Communication and the Law* (2d ed) Nashville: Abingdon Press, 1983.
Wigmore, John Henry, "Communications Between Priest and Penitent," in *Evidence in Trials at Common Law* (McNaughton) Boston: Little, Brown and Company, 1961.

Unpublished Materials

Glasow, Suzanne, "Confidentiality Within the Priest-Penitent Context," *Memorandum to Mark Chopko, USCC* (August 13, 1984).
Glasow, Suzanne, "Nondisclosure of Church Documents," *Memorandum to Mark Chopko, USCC* (August 20, 1985).
Glasow, Suzanne, "Recordkeeping and Record Retention Requirements in Diocesan Archives," *Memorandum to Mark Chopko, USCC* (August 13, 1985).
Krier, Donna M., "Confidential Communications: Civil Law Perspectives on the Canon Law Requirements," *Address Given to the Convention of the Midwest Canon Law Society* (April 29, 1987).
Krier, Donna M., "Confidentiality and Church Documents," *Address Given to Catholic Record Keeping in Modern America Conference* at The Catholic University of America (June 21, 1988).
Paprocki, Thomas J., "Clergy Malpractice and the Law," *Address Given to the Risk Management Conference, Montreal, Quebec, Canada* (September, 1986).
Serritella, James A., "Confidentiality and the Church," *Address Given to the Twenty-third National Meeting of the Diocesan Attorneys, Monterey, California* (April, 1987).
Serritella, James A., "The Civil Law and the Canonist: A Bifocal View," *Address Given to the Forty-first Convention of the Midwest Canon Law Society* (May 2, 1984).

STATUTES AND COURT DECISIONS OF THE FIFTY STATES

DONNA KRIER IOPPOLO

ALABAMA

The statute[1] limits the privilege to "any duly ordained, licensed or commissioned minister, pastor, priest, rabbi or practitioner of any bona fide established church or religious organization," and further limits it to those who devote "a substantial portion of his time" to the service of the religious organization. No case has defined this coverage, but the inclusion of those who are "commissioned" might be broadly interpreted.

The privilege is limited to "conversations with persons seeking confession, spiritual counsel or comfort, or advice in connection with marital problems." The Alabama court has limited these communications to those which are penitential[2], but it may cover marriage counseling when spouses seek the help of the clergy.

The statute allows the clergymen or the communicant to refuse disclosure and either may prevent the other from disclosing "anything said by either party during such communication."

The privilege applies in criminal or civil cases, grand jury proceedings, or hearings before administrative agencies.

Clergy are not among those required to report under the child abuse reporting statute.[3] However, like others, a clergyman may make such a report if reasonable cause exists or if they are called upon to render aid to any child.

Among the required reporters are physicians, school teachers and officials, social workers, day care workers, and mental health professionals. Clergy serving in these roles may be required reporters if information about child abuse or neglect comes to them in that capacity.

All privileges, except attorney-client, are not grounds for excluding evidence in any judicial proceeding.[4] Therefore, it appears the clergy privilege has been abrogated in these matters.

[1] Ala. code sec. 12-21-166 (1986 & Supp. 1987).

[2] *Lucy v. State,* 443 S.2d 1335 (Ala.Civ.App. 1983); *Santmier v. Santmier,* 494 So.2d 95 (Ala.Civ.App. 1986).

[3] Ala. Code sec. 26-14-3 (1986 & Supp. 1987).

[4] Ala. Code sec. 26-14-10 (1986 & Supp. 1987).

ALASKA

The clergy privilege[1] was added to the Rules of Evidence by an Alaska Supreme Court order. The rule defines clergyman as a "minister, priest, rabbi, or other similar functionary of a religious organization." It also includes a person "reasonably believed to be so by the person consulting him." "Other similar functionary" may provide room for expansion of the rule to cover a variety of ministries, however, no case has defined the scope of these terms.

A communication is confidential if "made privately and not intended for further disclosure except to other persons present in furtherance of the purpose of the communication." The statute appears to include all forms of pastoral counseling within its scope, including marriage counseling with both spouses present. The privilege is broadly applicable to all confidential communications within the clergyman's professional character as a spiritual advisor.

The privilege primarily belongs to the communicating person. However, the clergyman may claim the privilege on behalf of the person by authority of the discipline of the relevant church.

The rules of privilege apply at all stages of all actions, causes, and proceedings.

Clergy are not among those specifically required to report suspected child abuse or neglect.[2] However, like others, they may make such reports if they have reason to believe a child has been abused. Among required reporters are practitioners of the healing arts, school teachers and administrators, social workers, and licensed day care providers. Clergy who serve in these capacities may be required reporters if the information about child abuse comes to them in that capacity.

The statute specifically abrogates the physician-patient and husband-wife privilege.[3] Statutory construction implies that the clergy privilege may still be in effect in this matter, though no cases have clarified this interpretation.

[1] Alaska R. of Evid. 506 (1988).
[2] Alaska Stat. sec. 47.17.020 (1984).
[3] Alaska Stat. sec. 47.17.060 (1984).

ARIZONA

Arizona's separate statutes for civil[1] and criminal[2] cases are identically worded. Neither statute has been examined by the courts.

Both statutes are applicable to a "clergyman or priest" and are relevant to "any confession made to him in his character as clergyman or priest in the course of discipline enjoined by the church to which he belongs." Because the statute is limited to confessions, other kinds of communication, such as pastoral counseling, may not be covered.

The clergyman may not be examined "without the consent of the person making the confession." This would indicate that the penitent holds the privilege. It is not clear whether the clergyman can claim the privilege if the penitent waives it.

The privilege applies to civil actions and criminal cases. No mention is made of other administrative proceedings.

Clergy are not among those specifically mentioned as required reporters of abused and neglected children.[3] However, they may report such abuse or neglect, as may anyone, if they have reasonable grounds for such belief.

Among the required reporters are physicians, psychologists, school personnel, and social workers. Clergy who serve in these capacities may be required reporters if the information on child abuse comes to them in that capacity.

After abrogating all privileges in matters of child abuse, the Arizona legislature has specifically reinstated the clergy privilege in any civil or criminal litigation on these matters.[4] They have also extended the privilege to cases on abuse of the elderly.[5]

[1] Ariz. Rev. Stat. Ann. sec. 12-2233 (1982 & Supp. 1987).
[2] Ariz. Rev. Stat. Ann. sec. 13-4062 (1978 & Supp. 1987).
[3] Ariz. Rev. Stat. Ann. sec. 13-3620 (1978 & Supp. 1987).
[4] Ariz. Rev. Stat. Ann. sec. 8-546.04 (1974 & Supp. 1987).
[5] Ariz. Rev. Stat. Ann. sec. 46-453 (1988).

ARKANSAS

The rule[1] defines clergyman as a "minister, priest, rabbi, accredited Christian Science practitioner or other similar functionary of a religious organization." It also includes a person "reasonably believed so to be by the person consulting him." "Other similar functionary" may provide room for expansion of the rule to cover a variety of ministries, however, no case in Arkansas has defined the scope of these terms.

A communication is confidential if "made privately and not intended for further disclosure except to other persons present in furtherance of the purpose of the communication." This apparently allows the privilege to cover marriage counseling with both spouses present. However, where a confession is made to a great number of people as well as to a minister, the communicant has waived the right to have the confession to the minister remain privileged.[2] The privilege is broadly applicable to all confidential communications within the clergyman's professional character as a spiritual advisor.

The privilege primarily belongs to the communicating person. The clergyman "is presumed to have authority to claim the privilege, but only on behalf of the communicant." It appears that the clergyman will be compelled to testify in the face of waiver by the communicant.

The privilege rule applies to all proceedings in the courts of Arkansas and in grand jury proceedings. It apparently does not apply to administrative hearings.

Clergy are not among those specifically required to report suspected child abuse or neglect.[3] However, like others, they may make such a report if they have reasonable cause to suspect a child has been abused or neglected.

Among the required reporters are physicians, teachers, school officials, social service workers, foster care workers, and mental health professionals. Clergy serving in these roles may be required reporters if information about child abuse or neglect comes to them in that capacity.

The statute[4] specifically abrogates the clergy privilege in "any *proceeding* regarding child abuse, sexual abuse, or neglect of a child or the cause thereof." (emphasis added) It is not clear whether the privilege extends to the *reporting* of such abuse if a clergyman should fall into one of the mandatory reporting categories. No cases have yet dealt with this issue.

[1] Ark. R. of Evid. 505 (Michie 1988).
[2] *Perry v. State,* 280 Ark. 36, 655 S.W.2d 380.
[3] Ark. Code Ann. sec. 12-12-504 (1987 & Supp. 1987).
[4] Ark. Code Ann. 12-12-511 (1987 & Supp. 1987).

CALIFORNIA

The statute[1] limits the privilege to "a priest, minister, religious practitioner, or other similar functionary of a church or of a religious denomination or religious organization." "Other similar functionary" may provide room for expansion of the privilege to a variety of ministries, however, no case has defined the scope of these terms.

The statute covers "penitential communications (which) means a communication made in confidence, in the presence of no third person so far as the penitent is aware, to a clergyman who, in the course of the discipline or practice of his church..., is authorized or accustomed to hear such communications and, under the discipline or tenets of his church..., has a duty to keep such communications secret. A communication characterized as seeking counseling and not absolution was held not to be privileged.[2] Marriage counseling was held not privileged although an express agreement between the clergyman and the couple that their conversation would be confidential was upheld.[2] The communications must be made in confidence or in the course of the required relationship[4] and in order to receive religious consolation.[5] A clergyman may testify to the state of mind of a communicant.[6]

The privilege may be claimed by the penitent[7] and by the clergyman[8] and waiver by the penitent cannot compel the clergyman's testimony.

The privilege shall "apply in all proceedings" and commentary indicates this includes judicial and adjudicatory proceedings.[9] A recent holding limits the privilege to testimonial as opposed to extrajudicial statements.[10]

Clergy are not among those required to report under the child abuse reporting act.[11] However, like others they may make such a report if they have "knowledge of or observe a child whom he or she knows or reasonably suspects has been a victim of child abuse."

Among required reporters are physicians, psychiatrists, psychologists, marriage and family counselors, teachers, school administrative officers, administrators of child day care facilities and social workers. Clergy serving in these roles may be required reporters if information about child abuse or neglect comes to them in that capacity.

There is no mention of abrogation of privileges in the child abuse statute consequently the clergy privilege is apparently effective.

[1] Cal. Evid. Code sec. 1030 (West 1966 & Supp. 1988).
[2] *People v. Edwards,* 248 Cal. Rptr. 53 (1988).
[3] *Simrin v. Simrin,* 233 Cal. App. 2d 90, 43 Cal. Rptr. 376 (1965).
[4] *People v. Johnson,* 270 Cal. App. 2d 204, 75 Cal. Rptr. 605 (1969).
[5] *People v. Thompson,* 133 Cal. App. 3d 419, 184 Cal. Rptr. 72 (1982).
[6] *In re Toomes' Estate,* 54 Cal. 5609 (1880).
[7] Cal. Evid. Code sec. 1033 (West 1966 & Supp. 1988).
[8] Cal. Evid. Code sec. 1032 (West 1966 & Supp. 1988).
[9] Cal. Evid. Code sec. 910 (West 1966 & Supp. 1988).
[10] *People v. Edwards,* 248 Cal. Rptr. 53 (1988).
[11] Cal. Penal Code sec. 11166 (1982 & Supp. 1988).

COLORADO

The statute[1] limits the privilege to "a clergyman, minister, priest or rabbi." No case has defined these terms.

The statute covers "confidential communications made to [the clergyman] in his professional capacity in the course of discipline expected by the religious body to which he belongs." Cases[2] decided under the prior statute limit the application to situations where the clergyman and communicant are members of the same faith, the clergyman serves as the communicant's spiritual advisor, and the communication must be made in the course of spiritual advice or counsel.

The privilege is held by both the clergyman and communicant and the clergyman "shall not be examined without both his consent and also the consent of the person making the communication."

The privilege is limited to court proceedings.[3]

Clergy are not among those required to report under the child abuse reporting statute.[4] However, like others, they "may report known or suspected child abuse or neglect and circumstances or conditions which might reasonably result in child abuse or neglect."

Among required reporters are physicians, public or private school officials and employees, social workers, psychologists, and mental health professionals. Clergy serving in these roles may be required reporters if information about child abuse or neglect comes to them in that capacity.

The statute[5] abrogates the physician-patient, nurse-patient, and husband-wife privileges in these cases. The clergy privilege is still effective in these matters.

[1] Colo. Rev. Stat. sec. 13-90-107(1)(c) (1987 and amendment July 1, 1988).

[2] *Milburn v. Haworth*, 47 Colo. 593, 108 P. 155 (1910); *Mitsunaga v. People*, 54 Colo. 102, P. 241 (1913); *People v. Police*, 651 P. 2d 430 (Colo. App. 1982).

[3] Colo. Rev. Stat. sec. 13-90-107(1) (1987).

[4] Colo. Rev. Stat. sec. 19-3-304 (1986 & Supp. 1987).

[5] Colo. Rev. Stat. sec. 19-3-311 (1986 & Supp. 1987).

CONNECTICUT

The privilege statute[1] includes in its coverage "clergyman, priest, minister, rabbi, or practitioner of any religious denomination accredited by the religious body to which he belongs." The statute also requires that the clergyman be "settled in the work of the ministry." No cases have further defined the scope of this statute.

The privilege includes "confidential communications made to him in his professional capacity." This may be broadly interpreted to cover all forms of communication including counseling.

The statute states the clergyman "shall not disclose" a confidential communication "unless the person making the confidential communication waives such privilege." In one case it appeared the court was willing to call a priest as a witness if the defendant would waive the privilege.[2] Since the defendant refused to waive it, the priest was not called. It is not clear whether or not the court would have allowed the priest himself to claim the privilege.

The privilege may be claimed in any "civil or criminal case or proceedings preliminary thereto, or in any legislative or administrative hearing."

Clergymen are among those required to report under the child abuse reporting statute when reasonable cause of child abuse exists.[3] Other required reporters are school teachers, principals, and guidance counselors, social workers, and mental health professionals.

The abuse statute does not contain the abrogation of the statutory privileges in child abuse matters. It would appear, then, that the clergy may be required to report child abuse, but not required to testify in a subsequent proceeding on the matter.

[1] Conn. Gen. Stat. Ann. sec. 52-146(b) (1960 & Supp. 1988).
[2] *State v. Paluga,* 171 Conn. 586, 370 A.2d 1049 (1976).
[3] Conn. Gen. Stat. Ann. sec. 17-38a (1988).

DELAWARE

The privilege in Delaware is part of the Uniform Rules of Evidence.[1] The rule limits the privilege to a "minister, priest, rabbi, accredited Christian Science practitioner or other similar functionary of a religious organization." It also includes a person "reasonably believed so to be by the person consulting him." "Other similar functionary" may provide room for expansion of the rule to cover a variety of ministries, however, no case in Delaware has specifically defined this coverage.

A communication is confidential "if made privately and not intended for further disclosure except to other persons present in furtherance of the purpose of the communication." This would apparently allow for a privilege covering marriage counseling with both spouses present. It covers communications made "to a clergyman in his professional character as a spiritual advisor." In interpreting the Delaware rules, a federal court determined that the privilege did not cover a subpoena of a priests' personnel file merely on the basis "of a special relationship between a Bishop and his priest."[2] To be privileged, proof must be made that those documents are communications *from* the priest to his Bishop and disclosed to the Bishop "in his professional character as a spiritual advisor."

The privilege may be claimed by the communicant or the clergyman, whose authority to do so "is presumed in the absence of evidence to the contrary."

The privilege is applicable in all court proceedings, grand jury proceedings, and preliminary hearings in criminal cases.

Clergy are not among those specifically required to report suspected child abuse or neglect.[3] However, like others, they may make such a report if they have reasonable cause to suspect a child has been abused or neglected.

Among required reporters are physicians, school employees, social workers, and psychologists. Clergy serving in these roles may be required reporters if information about child abuse or neglect comes to them in that capacity.

All privileges, except attorney-client, have been abrogated in civil or criminal litigation regarding child abuse or in "any judicial proceeding resulting from a report submitted" under this statute.[4] It would appear this abrogation includes the clergy privilege.

[1] Del. R. of Evid. 505 (1987).
[2] *Pagano v. Hadley,* 100 F.R.D. 758 (1984).
[3] Del. Code. Ann. tit. 16, sec. 903 (1983 & Supp. 1986).
[4] Del. Code. Ann. tit. 16, sec. 908 (1983 & Supp. 1986).

DISTRICT OF COLUMBIA

The statute[1] limits the privilege to a "priest, clergyman, rabbi, or other duly licensed, ordained, or consecrated minister of a religion authorized to perform a marriage ceremony in the District of Columbia or duly accredited practitioner of Christian Science." No case has defined the scope of these terms.

The statute covers communications "made to him in his professional capacity in the course of confessions, religious or spiritual advice or in connection with an effort to reconcile estranged spouses." Marriage counseling with both spouses present would be included under the privilege.

The clergy cannot be examined as witnesses "without the consent of the person making the communication." In one case decided before the statute was enacted, a Lutheran minister's testimony was excluded because the defendant had not waived the privilege.[2] This was true even though the defendant's confession was not required by the discipline of the Lutheran Church. Neither statute nor cases address whether the clergyman will be compelled to testify when the communicant waives the privilege.

The privilege can be claimed "in any civil or criminal proceedings in the Federal courts . . . and District of Columbia courts." It does not appear to apply to other administrative hearings.

Clergy are not among those who are required reporters under the child abuse reporting statute.[3] However, like others, they may make such a report if they have reasonable cause to suspect a child has been abused or neglected.

Among required reporters are physicians, school officials and teachers, social service workers, and mental health professionals. Clergy serving in these roles may be required reporters if information about child abuse or neglect comes to them in that capacity.

The statute[4] specifically abrogates the physician-patient and husband-wife privileges in these cases. The clergy privilege is, apparently, effective in such proceedings.

[1] D.C. Code Ann. sec. 14-309 (1981 & Supp. 1987).
[2] *Mullen v. U.S.,* 105 U.S.APP. 25, 263 F.2d 275 (1958).
[3] D.C. Code Ann. sec. 2-1352 (1981 & Supp. 1987).
[4] D.C. Code Ann. sec. 2-1355 (1981 & Supp. 1987).

FLORIDA

The statute[1] defines a clergyman as "a priest, rabbi, practitioner of Christian Science, or minister of any religious organization or denomination usually referred to as a church." It also includes "an individual reasonably believed so to be by the person consulting him." No case has defined the scope of these terms.

Under the statute, a communication is confidential "if made privately for the purpose of seeking spiritual counsel and advice from the clergyman in the usual course of his practice or discipline and not intended for further disclosure except to other persons present in furtherance of the communication." The statute would appear to include all forms of pastoral counseling within its scope, including marriage counseling with both spouses present. However, communications made to a minister with the intention they conveyed to a third party are not privileged.[2]

The privilege may be claimed by the communicant or by the clergyman, on behalf of the communication, whose "authority to do so is presumed in the absence of evidence to the contrary."

The privilege is applicable in civil and criminal cases as well as grand jury proceedings and preliminary hearings.

Clergy are not among those required to report under the child abuse reporting statute.[3] However, like others, they may make such a report if they "know ( ), or (have) reasonable cause to suspect, that a child is an abused or neglected child."

Among required reporters are physicians; mental health professionals; school teachers, officials, or personnel; and social workers. Clergy serving in these roles may be required reporters if information about child abuse or neglect comes to them in that capacity.

Following the case of Rev. John Mellish,[4] held in contempt of court and jailed for refusing to testify in a child abuse matter, the Florida legislature enacted a statute restoring the clergy privilege in such cases.[5] The privilege has been restored in cases involving abuse of the elderly and handicapped.[6]

[1] Fla. Stat. Ann. sec. 90.505 (West 1979 & Supp. 1986).

[2] *Bottoson v. State,* 443 So.2d 962 (Fla. 1983), *cert. denied,* 469 U.S. 878 (1984).

[3] Fla. Stat. Ann. sec. 415.504 (West 1986 & Supp. 1988).

[4] Menendez, "Clergy Confidential: Confession May Be Good for the Soul, But It's a Problem for the State," 39 *Church and State,* 128 (1986); Scott, "Confidentiality in Child Abuse: Church and State Collide," 103 *The Christian Century* 174 (Feb. 19, 1986); Ostling, "Confidence and the Clergy," 124 *Time* 66 (Oct. 1, 1984).

[5] Fla. Stat. Ann. sec. 415.512 (West 1986 & Supp. 1988)

[6] Fla. Stat. Ann. sec. 415.109 (West 1986 & Supp. 1988).

GEORGIA

The statute[1] limits the privilege to "any Protestant minister of the Gospel, any priest of the Roman Catholic faith, any priest of the Greek Orthodox Catholic faith, any Jewish rabbi, or to any Christian or Jewish minister by whatever name called." No cases have further defined these terms, however, it is unlikely the privilege can be constitutionally limited to the Jewish and Christian faiths.

The statute covers "every communication made... professing religious faith, seeking spiritual comfort, or seeking counseling." Cases[2] limit application of the privilege to communications made in the course of spiritual comfort or counseling. The statute would appear to include all forms of pastoral counseling within its scope.

The privilege is held by the clergyman who cannot be compelled to testify regardless of waiver by the communicant.

The privilege is limited to court proceedings.

Clergy are not among those who are required to report under the child abuse reporting statute.[3] However, like others, they may make such a report if they have reasonable cause to suspect a child has been abused or neglected.

Among required reporters are physicians, psychologists, social work personnel, and school teachers, administrators, and guidance counsellors. Clergy serving in these roles may be required reporters if information about child abuse or neglect comes to them in that capacity.

There is no mention in the child abuse statute of the use or abrogation of privileges in these proceedings. Consequently, it can be assumed that the clergy privilege will apply in court proceedings.

[1] Ga. Code Ann. sec. 38-419.1 (1981 & Supp. 1986).

[2] *Burger v. State,* 238 Ga. 171, 231 S.E.2d 769 (1977); *Jones v. Department of Human Resources,* 168 Ga.App. 915, 310 S.E.2d 753 (1983).

[3] Ga. Code Ann. sec. 19-7-5 (1982 & Supp. 1985 & 1986).

HAWAII

The rule[1] defines clergyman as a "minister, priest, rabbi, Christian Science practitioner, or other similar functionary of a religious organization." It also includes "an individual reasonably believed so to be by the person consulting him." "Other similar functionary" may provide room for expansion of the rule to cover a variety of ministries, however, no case in Hawaii has specifically defined this coverage.

A communication is confidential if "made privately and not intended for further disclosure except to other persons present in furtherance of the purpose of the communication." This apparently allows the privilege to cover marriage counseling with both spouses present. The privilege is broadly applicable to all confidential communications made to "a clergyman in his professional character as a spiritual advisor."

The privilege may be claimed by the communicant or the clergyman, whose authority to do so "is presumed in absence of evidence to the contrary."

The privilege is applicable in all court proceedings and at all stages of all actions, cases, and proceedings.

Clergy are not among those required to report under the child abuse reporting statute.[2] However, like others, they may make such a report if they have reason to believe child abuse or neglect has occurred or that a substantial risk of such exists.

Among required reporters are physicians, psychologists, employees and officers of any public or private school, and employees and officers of any licensed child care facility or foster home. Clergy serving in these roles may be required reporters if information about child abuse or neglect comes to them in that capacity.

The statute[3] specifically abrogates the physician-patient psychologist-client, and husband-wife privileges in child abuse cases. The clergy privilege is apparently still effective in these matters.

[1] Hawaii Rev. Stat. tit. 33, ch. 626, R. of Evid. 506 (1985 & Supp. 1987).
[2] Hawaii Rev. Stat. tit. 20, sect. 350-1.1 (1985 & Supp. 1987).
[3] Hawaii Rev. Stat. tit. 20, sec. 350-5 (1985 & Supp. 1987).

IDAHO

The statute[1] limits the privilege to "a clergyman or priest." No cases have further defined the scope of these terms.

The statute covers "confessions... made to him in his professional character in the course of discipline enjoined by the church to which he belongs." A court decision limits the application to situations in which the communicant is a member of the clergyman's faith.[2] Communications made during conversations in the course of friendly meetings are not privileged. Because the statute is limited to confessions, other kinds of communication, such as pastoral counseling, may not be covered. No cases have yet determined the extent of the communications to be covered.

The privilege may be waived by the communicant. Neither statute nor cases address whether the clergyman will be compelled to testify when the communicant waives the privilege.

The privilege is limited to court proceedings.

Clergy are not among those specifically required to report suspected child abuse or neglect.[3] However, like others, they may make such a report if they have reasonable cause to suspect a child has been abused or neglected.

Among required reporters are physicians, school teachers, social workers, and day care personnel. Clergy serving in these roles may be required reporters if information about child abuse or neglect comes to them in that capacity.

The statute[4] specifically abrogates the clergy privilege "at any proceeding regarding the abuse, abandonment or neglect of the child or the cause thereof." Because this abrogation refers to "proceedings," it may not apply to the reporting of such abuse, but would apply to subsequent administrative hearings and court proceedings.

[1] Idaho Code sec. 9-203(3) (1979 & Supp. 1987).
[2] *Angleton v. Angleton,* 84 Idaho 184, 370 P.2d 788 (1962).
[3] Idaho Code sec. 16-1619 (1948 & Supp. 1987).
[4] Idaho Code sec. 16-1620 (Supp. 1987).

ILLINOIS

The statute[1] limits the privilege to "a clergyman or practitioner of any religious denomination accredited by the religious body to which he or she belongs." No case has defined the scope of these terms.

The statute covers "a confession or admission made to him or her in his or her professional character or as a spiritual advisor in the course of the discipline enjoined by the rules or practices of such religious body or of the religion which he or she professes, nor be compelled to divulge any information which has been obtained by him or her in such professional character or as such spiritual advisor." The statute has been held to include marriage counseling within its scope,[2] however, a communication made in the presence of a third party who was merely a listener was held not privileged.[3] The clergyman may reveal observations made, such as the physical or mental condition of the communicant without waiving the privilege as to the substance of the communication.[4]

The privilege is held by the clergyman. If he waives it, the burden is on the person claiming it to show that the disclosure is enjoined by the practice of the relevant religion.[5]

The privilege is applicable to disclosures "in any court, or to any administrative board or agency or to any public officer."

Clergy are not among those required to report under the child abuse reporting statute.[6] However, like others, they may make such a report if they have "reasonable cause to believe a child may be an abused child or a neglected child."

Among required reporters are physicians, school personnel, social workers, social services administrators, registered psychologists, and psychiatrists. Clergy serving in these roles may be required reporters if information about child abuse or neglect comes to them in that capacity. In addition, the "privileged quality of communication between any professional person required to report and his patient or client shall not apply to situations involving abused or neglected children."

The clergy privilege is effective in child abuse cases generally. However, if a clergyman becomes a required reporter by serving in a capacity making him so, "no evidence shall be excluded by reason of any... statutory privilege relating to communications between the alleged perpetrator of abuse or neglect, or the child subject of the report... and the person making... the report.[7]

[1] Ill. Ann. Stat. ch. 110, par. 8-803 (Smith-Hurd 1984 & Supp. 1988).
[2] *People v. Pecora,* 107 Ill. App. 2d 283, 246 N.E.2d 865 (1969); *cert. denied,* 397 U.S. 1028.
[3] *People v. Diercks,* 88 Ill. App. 3d 1073, 411 N.E.2d 97 (1980).
[4] *Snyder v. Poplett,* 98 Ill. App. 3d 359, 424 N.E.2d 396 (1981).
[5] *People v. Diercks,* 88 Ill. App. 3d 1073, 411 N.E.2d 97 (1980).
[6] Ill. Ann. Stat. ch. 23, par. 2054 (Smith-Hurd 1988).
[7] Ill. Ann. Stat. ch. 23, par. 2060 (Smith-Hurd 1988).

INDIANA

The statute[1] states that "clergymen" are not competent as witnesses. No case has defined the scope of this term.

The statute covers "confessions or admissions made to them in the course of discipline enjoined by their respective churches." A court decision permits clergy to testify on the "soundness of mind" of a communicant[2] or to communications made in non-religious situations.[3] Because the statute is limited to confessions or admissions, other kinds of communication, such as pastoral counseling, may not be covered.

Since the statute declares clergymen to be incompetent witnesses, waiver by the penitent does not destroy the privilege.

The privilege appears to cover all proceedings in which clergy can be called as "witnesses".

Clergy are not among those required to report under the child abuse reporting statute.[4] However "any individual who has reason to believe that a child is a victim of child abuse or neglect shall make a report."

Among required reporters are physicians, mental health professionals, social workers, and members of the staff of a public or private institution, school, facility or agency. Clergy serving in these roles may be required reporters if information about child abuse or neglect comes to them in that capacity.

The statute abrogates privilege communications between a husband

and wife and a health care provider and patient.[5] The clergy privilege is apparently still effective in these matters.

[1] Ind. Code Ann. sec. 34-1-14-5 (Burns 1986 & Supp. 1988).
[2] *Buuck v. Kruckeberg,* 121 Ind. App. 262, 95 N.E.2d 304 (1951).
[3] *Gillooley v. State,* 58 Ind. 182 (1877); *Farner v. Farner,* 480 N.E.2d 251 (Ind. App. 1985).
[4] Ind. Code Ann. 31-6-11-3 (Burns 1987 & Supp. 1988).
[5] Ind. Code Ann. 31-6-11-8 (Burns 1987 & Supp. 1988).

IOWA

The statute[1] limits the privilege to a "minister of the gospel or priest of any denomination." Case law has included within this definition ruling elders of the Presbyterian church when acting in their spiritual capacity according to church discipline.[2]

The statute covers "any confidential communication properly entrusted to the person in the person's professional capacity, and necessary and proper to enable the person to discharge the functions of the person's office according to the usual course of practice or discipline." The Iowa courts have included marital counseling as a communication covered by the privilege[3] as well as observations.[4] A federal court interpreting the Iowa statute has extended the privilege to testimony of the parties and the wirnesses in the course of Catholic annulment proceedings.[5]

The privilege may be waived by the communicant. Neither statute nor cases address whether the clergyman will be compelled to testify when the communicant waives the privilege.

The privilege covers all "giving testimony" in proceedings.

Clergy are not among those required to report under the child abuse reporting statute.[6] However, like others, they may make such a report if they believe that a child has been abused.

Among required reporters are health practitioners, social workers, psychologists, school employees, employees or operators or licensed child care centers, counselors, and mental health professionals. Clergy serving in these roles may be required reporters if information about child abuse or neglect comes to them in that capacity.

The statute[7] abrogates privileges covered in the statutory section which includes the clergy privilege, but does not specifically mention the clergy privilege. It is therefore unclear whether or not the clergy privilege will apply in child abuse proceedings.

[1] Iowa Code Ann. sec. 622-10 (West 1950 & Supp. 1988).
[2] *Reutkemeier v. Nolte,* 179 Iowa 343, 161 N.W.2d 401 (1917).
[3] *Pardie v. Pardie,* 158 N.W.2d 641 (Iowa 1968).
[4] *Boyles v. Cora,* 232 Iowa 822, 6 N.W.2d 401 (1942).

[5] *Cimijotti v. Paulsen,* 219 F.Supp. 621 (N.D. Iowa 1963), *appeal dismissed,* 323 F.2d 716 (8th Cir. 1963), *on remand,* 230 F.Supp. 39 (N.D. Iowa 1964), *aff'd,* 340 F.2d 613 (8th Cir. 1965).

[6] Iowa Code Ann. 232.69 (West & Supp. 1988).

[7] Iowa Code Ann. sec. 232.74 (West 1985 & Supp. 1988).

KANSAS

The statute[1] limits the privilege to "a regular or duly ordained minister of religion." The statute defines the term "duly ordained minister of religion" to mean "a person who has been ordained, in accordance with the ceremonial ritual, or discipline of a church... to preach and to teach the doctrines of such church... and to administer the rites and ceremonies thereof in public worship." The term "regular minister of religion means one who as his or her customary vocation preaches and teaches the principles of religion of a church... without having been formally ordained... and who is recognized by such church... as a regular minister." This broad definition has not been further discussed by the courts.

The statute covers "any communication... which the penitent intends shall be kept secret and confidential and which pertains to advice or assistance in determining or discharging the penitent's moral obligations or to obtaining God's mercy or forgiveness for past culpable conduct." The statute would appear to include all forms of pastoral counseling within its scope.

The privilege is applicable to both criminal and civil proceedings conducted by or under the supervision of a court in which evidence is produced.

The privilege may be claimed by the penitent or minister if called as a witness or by the minister on behalf of an absent penitent.

Clergy are not among those who are required to report under the child abuse reporting statute.[2] However, like others, they may make such a report if they have reason to suspect that a child has been injured as a result of abuse or neglect.

Among required reporters are persons licensed to practice the healing arts, licensed psychologists, school administrators or other employees of a school, and licensed social workers. Clergy serving in these roles may be required reporters if information about child abuse or neglect comes to them in that capacity.

All proceedings in child abuse are to be governed by the Civil Procedure Act.[3] It can be assumed that the clergy privilege will apply in these proceedings.

[1] Kan. Stat. Ann. sec. 60-429 (1986 & Supp. 1987).

[2] Kan. Stat. Ann. sec. 38-1522 (1986 & Supp. 1987).

[3] Kan. Stat. Ann. sec. 60-3109 (1986 & Supp. 1987).

KENTUCKY

The statute[1] limits the privilege to "an ordained minister, priest, rabbi or accredited practitioner of an established church or religious organization." No cases have defined these terms, although it is unlikely the privilege can be constitutionally limited to an established church.

The statute covers "any information confidentially communicated to him in his professional capacity under such circumstances that to disclose the information would violate a sacred or moral trust." Cases reinforce that the communication must be made to the clergyman in his professional capacity.[2] The statute would appear to include all forms of pastoral counseling within its scope.

No clergyman shall testify "unless the person making the confidential communication waives such privilege." It is not clear whether a clergyman will be compelled to testify in face of such waiver.

The privilege is effective for "any civil or criminal case or proceedings preliminary thereto, or in any administrative proceeding."

Clergy are not among those required to report under the child abuse reporting statute.[3] However, like others, they may make such a report if they have reasonable cause to believe that a child has been abused or neglected.

Among required reporters are physicians, teachers, school personnel, social workers, child care personnel, and mental health professionals. Clergy serving in these roles may be required reporters if information about child abuse or neglect comes to them in that capacity.

After abrogating privileges in matters of child abuse, the Kentucky legislature has specifically reinstated the clergy privilege for both testifying in judicial proceedings and for reporting of abuse.

[1]Ky. Rev. Stat. Ann. sec. 421-210(4) (Bobbs-Merrill 1972 & Supp. 1986).

[2]*Johnson v. Commonwealth,* 310 Ky. 557, 221 S.W.2d 87 (1949); *Wainscott v. Commonwealth,* 562 S.W.2d 628 (Ky. 1978), *cert. denied,* 439 U.S. 868 (1978).

[3]Ky. Rev. Stat. Ann. sec. 199.335 (2) (Michie/Bobbs-Merrill 1982 & Supp. 1986).

LOUISIANA

Louisiana has separate statutes on clergy privilege for civil[1] and criminal[2] cases. The civil procedure statute limits the privilege to "clergymen, duly ordained minister of the gospel or ordained priest." The criminal procedure statute is limited to "clergymen." No cases have defined these terms, though self-ordained ministers have been excluded from coverage.[3]

Both statutes include "any communication made to him by any person seeking his spiritual advice or consolation, or relative to any information he may have obtained by reason of such communication."

Cases hold that the communication be made to the clergyman in his professional capacity.[4] The statute appears to include all forms of pastoral counseling within its scope.

Both statutes place the ownership of the privilege in the hands of the communicant. The civil statute indicates that the clergyman will be compelled to testify if the privilege is waived. The criminal statute states that if waived "the clergyman... may be examined and cross-examined to the same extent as any other witness."

The privilege extends to civil and criminal proceedings.

A separate statute[5] protects communications, documents, and evidence gathered relating to the determination by religious authorities of the validity of marriages.

"Priests, rabbis, duly ordained ministers, or Christian Science practitioners" are specifically excluded as reporters under the child abuse reporting statute.[6] However, like others, they may make such a report if they have cause to believe a child's physical or mental health or welfare is in danger.

Among required reporters are health practitioners, mental health/social service practitioners and teaching or child care providers including principals, school staff members, and child care institution staff members. Clergy serving in these roles may be required reporters if information about child abuse or neglect comes to them in that capacity.

After abrogating all privileges in matters of child abuse, the Louisiana legislature has specifically reinstated the clergy privilege in these proceedings.

[1]La. Rev. Stat. Ann. sec. 13:3734.1 (West 1968 & Supp. 1988).

[2]La. Rev. Stat. Ann. sec. 15:477 (West 1981 & Supp. 1988).

[3]*State v. Welch,* 448 So.2d 705 (La.App. 1984), *cert. denied,* 450 So.2d 952 (La. 1984).

[4]*State v. Berry,* 324 So.2d 822 (La. 1975), *cert. denied, 425 U.S. 954 (1976); State v. Hereford,* 518 So.2d 515 (La. App. 1987).

[5]La. Rev. Stat. Ann. sec. 13:3734.2 (West 1968 & Supp. 1988).

[6]La. Rev. Stat. Ann. sec. 14:403B (West 1986 & Supp. 1988).

MAINE

The rule of evidence covering religious privilege[1] defines a clergyman as "a minister, priest, rabbi, accredited Christian Science practitioner, or other similar functionary of a religious organization." It also includes "an individual reasonably believed so to be by the person consulting him." "Other similar functionary" may provide room for expansion of the rule to cover a variety of ministries, however, no case in Maine has further defined this coverage.

"A communication is confidential if made privately and not intended for further disclosure except to other persons present in furtherance of the purpose of the communication." The privilege is applicable to all confidential communications made to "a clergyman in his professional capacity as a spiritual advisor." The statute would appear to include all forms of pastoral counseling within its scope, including marriage counseling with both parties present.

The privilege may be claimed by the communicant or the clergyman who "is presumed to have authority to claim the privilege but only on behalf of the communicant."

The privilege is applicable in all actions and proceedings, including grand juries.

Clergy are not among those required to report under the child abuse reporting statute.[2] However, like others, they may make such a report if they "know or have reasonable cause to suspect that a child has been or is likely to be abused or neglected."

Among required reporters are physicians, teachers, guidance counselors, school officials, social workers, psychologists, and other mental health professionals. Clergy serving in these roles may be required reporters if information about child abuse or neglect comes to them in that capacity.

The statute[3] abrogates physician-patient and husband-wife privileges in child abuse cases. The clergy privilege is apparently still effective in these matters.

[1]Me. R. of Evid. 505 (1988).
[2]Me. Rev. Stat. Ann. tit. 22, sec. 4011 (West 1980 & Supp. 1987).
[3]Me. Rev. Stat. Ann. tit. 22, sec. 4015 (West 1980 & Supp. 1987).

MARYLAND

The statute[1] limits the privilege to "a minister of the gospel, clergyman, or priest of an established church of any denomination." No cases have defined these terms, although it is unlikely the privilege can be constitutionally limited to an established church.

The statute covers "any matter in relation to any confession or communication made to him in confidence by a person seeking his spiritual advice or consolation." The statute would appear to include pastoral counseling within its scope.

The clergyman holds the privilege and "may not be compelled to testify," presumably even in the face of waiver by the communicant.

The privilege is effective in all judicial proceedings.

Clergy are not among those required to report under the child abuse reporting statute.[2] However, like others, they should make such a report if they have "reason to believe that a child has been subjected to abuse."[3] This statute, though lacking in sanctions or penalties, is "intended to be mandatory and applicable to all citizens."

Among required reporters are health practitioners, educators, and social workers. Clergy serving in these roles may be required reporters if information about child abuse or neglect comes to them in that capacity.

The statute abrogates "any law on privileged communications," though this may be read to apply only to those specifically designated as required reporters. It is not clear whether the clergy privilege is applicable in child abuse cases.

[1]Md. Cts. & Jud. Proc. Code Ann. sec. 9-111 (1984 & Supp. 1987).
[2]Md. Fam. Law Code Ann. sec. 5-903 (1984 & Supp. 1987).
[3]Md. Fam. Law Code Ann. sec. 5-904 (1984 & Supp. 1987).

MASSACHUSETTS

The statute[1] limits the privilege to a "priest, rabbi or ordained or licensed minister of any church or an accredited Christian Science practitioner." No cases have defined the scope of these terms.

The statute covers "a confession made to him in his professional character, in the course of discipline enjoined by the rules or practice of the religious body to which he belongs" or "a communication made to him by any person in seeking religious or spiritual advice or comfort, or as to his advice given thereon in the course of his professional duties or in his professional character." The statute would appear to include all forms of pastoral ministry within its scope. Further, in holding that the showing of a gun to a minister during the course of a privileged communication was also privileged, the Massachusetts court stated, "a communication is not limited to conversation and includes other acts by which ideas may be transmitted from one person to another."[2]

The communicant holds the privilege and the clergyman may not testify "without the consent of such person." Further, the Massachusetts court has held that when the communicant waives the privilege, the clergyman must testify and may be held in contempt of court if he does not.[3]

The privilege is effective in all judicial proceedings.

Clergy are not among those required to report under the child abuse reporting statute.[4] However, like others, they may make such a report if they have "reasonable cause to believe that a child is suffering from or has died as a result of such abuse or neglect."

Among required reporters are physicians, psychologists, school teachers, educational administrators, guidance counselors, and social workers. Clergy serving in these roles may be required reporters if information about child abuse or neglect comes to them in that capacity.

The statute[5] abrogates privileges for psychotherapists and social workers for both reporting and testifying. The clergy privilege is apparently effective in these matters.

[1]Mass. Gen. Laws Ann. ch. 223, sec. 20A (West 1986 & Supp. 1988).
[2]*Commonwealth v. Zezima*, 365 Mass. 238, 310 N.E.2d 590 (1974).
[3]*Commonwealth v. Kane*, 388 Mass. 128, 445 N.E.2d 598 (1983).
[4]Mass. Gen. Laws Ann. ch. 119, sec. 51a (West 1969 & Supp. 1988).
[5]*Id.*

MICHIGAN

The statute[1] limits the privilege to a "minister of the gospel, or priest of any denomination whatsoever, or duly accredited Christian Science practitioner." No cases have further defined these terms.

The statute covers "any confession made to him in his professional character, in the course of discipline enjoined by the rules or practice of such denomination." Because the statute is limited to confessions, other kinds of communication, such as pastoral counseling, may not be covered.

The privilege is held by the clergyman who shall not "be allowed to disclose", presumably even in the face of waiver by the communicant.

The privilege is effective in civil and criminal proceedings, including grand juries and other proceedings before trial.[2] Allowing a minister to testify during a trial as to the fact of a conversation, but not its content has been held to be reversible error.[3]

Clergy are not among those required to report under the child abuse reporting statute.[4] However, like others, they may make such a report if they "have reasonable cause to suspect child abuse or neglect."

Among required reporters are physicians, psychologists, family therapists, social workers, school administrators, and teachers. Clergy serving in these roles may be required reporters if information about child abuse or neglect comes to them in that capacity.

The statute[5] abrogates "any legally recognized privilege communication except that between attorney and client... and (such privileges) neither constitute grounds for excusing a report otherwise required to be made nor for excluding evidence in a civil child protective proceeding resulting from a report." No case has yet been decided on the clergy privilege in this context.

[1]Mich. Comp. Laws Ann. sec. 600.2156 (West 1986 & Supp. 1988).
[2]Mich. Comp. Laws Ann. sec. 767.5a (West 1982 & Supp. 1988).
[3]*Wirtanen v. Prudential Ins. Co. of America*, 27 Mich. App. 260, 183 N.W.2d 456 (1970).
[4]Mich. Comp. Laws Ann. sec. 722.623 (West 1968 & Supp. 1988).
[5]Mich. Comp. Laws Ann. sec. 722.631 (West 1968 & Supp. 1988).

MINNESOTA

The statute[1] limits the privilege to "a member of the clergy or other minister of any religion." A Minnesota court held this included "the spiritual advisor of any religion, whether he be termed priest, rabbi, clergyman, minister of the gospel, or any other official designation."[2] However, it does not include a person working under the direction of a priest.[3]

The statute covers "a confession made to the member of the clergy . . . in a professional character, in the course of discipline enjoined by the rules or practice of the religious body to which (he) belongs" or "to any communication made to (him) by any person seeking religious or spiritual advice, aid, or comfort or advice given thereon." The statute appears to include all forms of pastoral counseling within its scope. The Minnesota court held that the communication must be made in the course of seeking spiritual advice and with the expectation of confidentiality.[4]

The privilege is held by the communicant and the clergyman may be compelled to testify if the privilege is waived.[5]

The privilege applies to civil and criminal proceedings in court or before any person who has authority to receive evidence.

Clergy are required to report when they "know ( ) or (have) reason to believe a child is being neglected or physically or sexually abused," however, the statute provides "that a member of the clergy is not required to report information that is otherwise privileged."[6] Other required reporters include professionals in the practice of the healing arts, social services, education, and psychological treatment.

Although privileges have been abrogated for spouses, physicians, nurses, and psychologists, the clergy privilege is apparently effective for proceedings arising out of alleged child abuse.[7] It is not clear how this provision will work in conjunction with the mandatory reporting requirement. The clergy privilege has been abrogated in proceedings regarding the abuse or neglect of vulnerable adults.[8]

[1]Minn. Stat. Ann. sec. 595.02(1)(c) (West 1988).

[2]*In re Swenson,* 183 Minn. 602, 237 N.W. 589 (1931).

[3]*State v. Lender,* 266 Minn. 561, 124 N.W.2d 355 (1963).

[4]*Christensen v. Pestorious,* 189 Minn. 548, 250 N.W. 363 (1933); *State v. Black,* 291 N.W.2d 208 (Minn. 1980).

[5]*State v. Lender,* 266 Minn. 561, 124 N.W.2d 355 (1963).

[6]Minn. Stat. Ann. sec. 626.556(3) (West 1983 & Supp. 1988) as amended April 26, 1988.

[7]Minn. Stat. Ann. sec. 626.556(3) (West 1983 & Supp. 1988).

[8]Minn. Stat. Ann. sec. 626.577(8) (West 1983 & Supp. 1988).

MISSISSIPPI

The statute[1] defines a clergyman as "a minister, priest, rabbi, or other similar functionary of a church, religious organization, or religious denomination." No cases in Mississippi have defined the scope of these terms. Also covered under the statute[2] is "a clergyman's secretary, stenographer or clerk... (when) knowledge... was acquired in that capacity."

"A communication is confidential if made privately and not intended for further disclosure except in furtherance of the purpose of the communication." The statute would appear to include all forms of pastoral counseling within its scope, but marriage counseling with both spouses present may be excluded.

The privilege may be claimed by the communicant and by the clergyman only on behalf of the communicant, unless it is waived. Apparently, the clergyman may be compelled to testify if the privilege is waived.

The privilege is applicable in all courts.

"Ministers" (without further definition) are among those specifically required to report under the child abuse reporting statute[3] when they have "reasonable cause to suspect that a child is abused... or of whom he has knowledge through observation, is a neglected child or an abused child." Others included as required reporters are physicians, attorneys, psychologists, teachers, social workers, and school principals.

The abuse statute does not contain any references to the abrogation of privileges in child abuse matters, though it does make good faith reports immune from civil or criminal liability and states that such reports "shall not constitute a breach of confidentiality."[4] There are no cases clarifying this position.

[1]Miss. Code Ann. sec. 13-1-22(1)(a) (1972 & Supp. 1986).

[2]Miss. Code Ann. sec. 13-1-22(4) (1972 & Supp. 1986).

[3]Miss. Code Ann. sec. 43-21-353 (1981 & Supp. 1986); Miss. Code Ann. sec. 43-23-9 (1981 & Supp. 1986).

[4]Miss. Code Ann. sec. 43-23-9 (1981 & Supp. 1986).

MISSOURI

The statute[1] determines as "incompetent to testify... any person practicing as a minister of the gospel, priest, rabbi, or other person serving in a similar capacity for any organized religion." A federal court interpreting the Missouri statute[2] included in this definition a Catholic nun who served as a spiritual director, determining that she performed a number of priestly functions and that spiritual director is a recognized office in the Catholic Church.

The statute covers "a communication made to him in his professional capacity as a spiritual advisor, confessor, counselor or comforter." The statute appears to include all forms of pastoral counseling within its scope, though marriage counseling with both parties present may not be included. When communications are not made in the clergy's professional capacity, they are not privileged.[3] A clergyman may testify on his personal observations as to the communicant's state of mind.[4]

Since the statute declares clergy to be incompetent as witnesses, waiver by the communicant does not destroy the privilege.

The privilege is applicable in all proceedings in which clergy can be called as witnesses.

Clergy are not among those required to report under the child abuse reporting statute.[5] However, like others, they may make such a report if they have "reasonable cause to suspect that a child has been or may be subjected to abuse or neglect."

Among required reporters are physicians, psychologists, mental health professionals, social workers, teachers, principals and other school officials. Clergy serving in these roles may be required reporters if information about child abuse or neglect comes to them in that capacity.

The statute[6] abrogates all privileges, except attorney-client, for reporting and testimony in judicial proceedings. No cases have yet dealt with this issue.

[1] Mo. Ann. Stat. sec. 491-060(4) (Vernon 1952 & Supp. 1988).

[2] *Eckmann v. Board of Education of Hawthorn School Dist. No. 17,* 106 F.R.D. 70 (E.D. Mo. 1985).

[3] *State v. Morgan,* 196 Mo. 177, 95 S.W. 402 (1906); *Partridge v. Partridge,* 220 Mo. 321, 199 S.W. 415 (1909).

[4] *State v. Kurtz,* 564 S.W.2d 856 (Mo. 1978).

[5] Mo. Ann. Stat. sec. 210.115 (Vernon 1983 & Supp. 1988).

[6] Mo. Ann. Stat. sec. 210.140 (Vernon 1983 & Supp. 1988).

MONTANA

The statute[1] is limited to "a clergyman or priest." No case has defined the scope of these terms.

The statute covers "any confessions made to him in his professional character in the course of discipline enjoined by the church to which he belongs." Because the statute is limited to confessions, other kinds of communication, such as pastoral counseling, may not be covered.

The clergyman cannot testify "without the consent of the person making the confession." Neither statute nor cases address whether the clergyman will be compelled to testify when the communicant waives the privilege.

The privilege is applicable in all proceedings in which clergy can be called as witnesses.

Clergy are not among those required to report under the child abuse reporting statute.[2] However, like others, a clergyman may make such a report if he "knows or has reasonable cause to suspect that a child is abused or neglected."

Among required reporters are physicians, mental health professionals, school teachers and other school officials, and social workers. Clergy serving in these roles may be required reporters if information about child abuse or neglect comes to them in that capacity.

The statute abrogates the privileges of required reporters. The clergy privilege is, apparently, still effective in such proceedings.

[1] Mont. Code Ann. sec. 26-1-804 (1987).
[2] Mont. Code Ann. sec. 41-3-201(2) (1987).

NEBRASKA

The statute[1] limits the privilege to a clergyman, defined as "a minister, priest, rabbi, or other similar functionary of a religious organization." It also includes "an individual reasonably believed so to be by the person consulting him." Other similar functionary may provide room for expansion of the statute to cover a variety of ministries, however, no case has defined the scope of these terms.

"A communication is confidential if made privately and not intended for further disclosure except to other persons present in furtherance of the purposes of the communication." The privilege is applicable to all confidential communications made to "a clergyman in his professional character as a spiritual advisor." The statute would appear to include all forms of pastoral counseling within its scope including marriage counseling with both spouses present. Communications made to a clergyman and intended to be communicated to others are not privileged.[2]

The privilege may be claimed by the communicant or the clergyman whose "authority so to do is presumed in absence of evidence to the contrary."

The privilege applies at all stages of all actions, cases and proceedings.

The statute[3] requiring reports of abuse of neglect concerns "a child or an incompetent, or disabled person." While clergy are not specifically listed as required reporters, the statute mandates that "any other person (with) reasonable cause to believe" abuse or neglect exists shall report such an incident.

Among required reporters are physicians, school employees, and social workers. Clergy serving in these roles may be required reporters if information about child abuse or neglect comes to them in that capacity.

Although privileges have been abrogated between husband and wife and physician and patient,[4] the clergy privilege is, apparently, still effective for proceedings arising out of alleged child abuse. It would appear, then, that the clergy may be required to report abuse of children, incompetents, or the disabled, but not required to testify in subsequent proceedings.

[1] Neb. Rev. Stat. sec. 27-506 (1985 & Supp. 1985, 1986, 1987).
[2] *Hills v. State,* 61 Neb. 589, 85 N.W. 836 (1901).
[3] Neb. Rev. Stat. sec. 28-711 (1985 & Supp. 1986, 1987).
[4] Neb. Rev. Stat. sec. 28-714 (1985 & Supp. 1986, 1987).

NEVADA

The statute[1] includes in its coverage a "clergyman or priest." No cases have defined the scope of these terms.

The statute covers "any confession made to him in his professional character." Because the statute is limited to confessions, other kinds of communication, such as pastoral counseling, may not be covered.

The statute states the clergyman "shall not, without the consent of the person making the confession, be examined as a witness." No case has determined whether the clergyman can claim the privilege himself in face of waiver by the penitent.

The privilege applies to civil or criminal proceedings.

Clergy *are* required to report abused or neglected children "unless he has acquired the knowledge of the abuse or neglect from the offender during a confession."[2] Other required reporters include physicians, psychologists, marriage and family counselors, social workers and school teachers and counselors.

All privileges, including the clergy privilege, have been abrogated in matters relating to child abuse or neglect including reporting, agency investigations and subsequent judicial proceedings.

[1] Nev. Rev. Stat. sec. 49.255 (1985 & Supp. 1987).
[2] Nev. Rev. Stat. sec. 432B.230(2)(d) (1985 & Supp. 1987).

NEW HAMPSHIRE

The statute[1] limits the privilege to "a priest, rabbi or ordained or licensed minister of any church or a duly accredited Christian Science practitioner." No cases have defined the scope of these terms.

The statute covers "a confession or confidence made to him in his professional character as spiritual advisor." The statute appears to include all forms of pastoral counseling within its scope, though marriage counseling with both parties present may not be included.

The clergyman "shall not be required to disclose . . . unless the person confessing or confiding waives the privilege." No case has determined whether the clergyman will be compelled to testify in the face of such waiver.

The privilege applies to all court proceedings.

Clergy *are* required to report when they have "reason to suspect that a child has been abused or neglected.[2] Other required reporters include physicians, psychologists, teachers, school officials and counselors, and social workers.

The statute[3] abrogates "the privileged quality of communication between husband and wife and any professional person and his patient or client" for matters including reporting of child abuse or neglect and any subsequent judicial proceedings.

[1]N.H. Rev. Stat. Ann. sec. 516:35 (1974 & Supp. 1987).
[2]N.H. Rev. Stat. Ann. sec. 169-C:29 (1955 & Supp. 1987).
[3]N.H. Rev. Stat. Ann. sec. 169-C:32 (1955 & Supp. 1987).

NEW JERSEY

The statute[1] limits the privilege to "a clergyman, minister or other person or practitioner authorized to perform similar functions, of any religion." A New Jersey court refused to extend the privilege to a Catholic nun because she did not perform priestly functions.[2]

The statute covers "a confession or other confidential communication made to him in his professional character, or as a spiritual advisor in the course of the discipline or practice of the religious body to which he belongs or of the religion he professes, (or) . . . the confidential relations and communications between and among him and individuals, couples, families or groups with respect to the exercise of his professional counseling role." The statute includes all forms of pastoral counseling within its scope, including marriage counseling and group retreats and other similar programs.

The privilege is held by the clergyman who "shall not be allowed or compelled to disclose" even in the face of waiver by the communicant. However, the clergyman waives the privilege if he "without coercion and with knowledge of his right or privilege make(s) disclosure of any part of the privileged matter or consent(s) to such a disclosure made by anyone."[3]

The privilege "shall apply in all cases and to all proceedings, places, and inquiries, whether formal, informal, public or private, as well as to all branches of government."[4]

"Any person having reasonable cause to believe that a child has been subjected to child abuse or acts of child abuse shall report the same promptly."[5] There is no exclusion of the clergy as persons required to report.

After abrogating all privileges in matters of child abuse or neglect, the New Jersey legislature has reinstated all privileges.[6] It is not clear how this relates to the reporting requirements. Consequently, clergy are required reporters but may refuse to testify in subsequent proceedings.

[1]N.J. Stat. Ann. sec. 2A:84A-23 (West 1976 & Supp. 1988).

[2]*In re Murtha,* 115 N.J.Super. 380, 279 A.2d 889 (1971), *cert. denied,* 59 N.J. 239, 281 A.2d 278 (1971).

[3]N.J. Stat. Ann. sec. 2A:84A-29 (West 1976 & Supp. 1988).

[4]N.J. Stat. Ann. sec. 2A:84A-16, Rule 2 (West 1976 & Supp. 1988).

[5]N.J. Stat. Ann. sec. 9:6-8.10 (West 1976 & Supp. 1987).

[6]N.J. Stat. Ann. sec. 9:6-8.46 (West 1976 & Supp. 1987).

NEW MEXICO

The rule of evidence covering communications to clergymen[1] defines a clergyman as "a minister, priest, rabbi or other similar functionary of a religious organization." It also includes "an individual reasonably believed so to be by the person consulting him." "Other similar functionary" may provide room for expansion of the rule to cover a variety of ministries, however, no case has defined the scope of these terms.

"A communication is confidential if made privately and not intended for further disclosure except to other persons present in furtherance of the purpose of the communication." The privilege is applicable to confidential communications made "to a clergyman in his professional character as spiritual advisor." The statute appears to include all forms of pastoral counseling within its scope, including marriage counseling with both parties present.

The privilege may be claimed by the communicant or the clergyman whose "authority so to do is presumed in the absence of evidence to the contrary."

The privilege applies "at all stages of all actions, cases and proceedings.[2]

The child abuse and neglect reporting statute[3] requires "any ... person knowing or suspecting that a child is an abused or neglected child shall report the matter immediately." The statute apparently includes the clergy within its scope. Among the specifically named required reporters are physicians, school teachers and social workers.

All privileges, including the clergy privilege, have been abrogated in matters regarding child abuse or neglect.[4]

[1]N.M. Stat. Ann. Rule of Evid. 11-506 (Michie 1986 & Supp. 1987).

[2]N.M. Stat. Ann. Rules of Evid. 11-1101(c) (Michie 1986 & Supp. 1987).

[3]N.M. Stat. Ann. sec. 32-1-15 (Michie 1978 & Supp. 1986, 1987).

[4]N.M. Stat. Ann. sec. 32-1-16 (Michie 1978 & Supp. 1986, 1987).

NEW YORK

The statute[1] limits the privilege to "a clergyman, or other minister of any religion or duly accredited Christian Science practitioner." No cases have defined the scope of these terms, but the court refused to extend coverage under this section to social workers merely because they were employed by a religious institution.[2]

The statute covers "a confession or confidence made to him in his professional character as spiritual advisor." The statute appears to include all forms of pastoral counseling and the courts have indicated the statute is to be "accorded broad and liberal construction."[3] Marriage counseling is included within the statute's coverage.[4] The statute protects only those communications made in the course of seeking spiritual advice.[5] A priest's records regarding marriage counseling undertaken with a couple are not privileged when the couple places damage to their marital relationship at issue in a trial.[6]

The clergyman "shall not be allowed to disclose" a communication "(u)nless the person confessing or confiding waives the privilege." It appears that all waivers will compel the clergyman to testify. When both spouses who participated in marriage counseling waive the privilege, the clergyman cannot claim it independently and must testify.[7]

The privilege applies in all judicial proceedings.

Clergy are not among those required to report under the child abuse reporting statute.[8] However, like others, they "may make such a report if (they) ha(ve) reasonable cause to suspect that a child is an abused or maltreated child.[9]

Among required reporters are physicians, psychologists, school officials, social services workers, and mental health professionals. Clergy serving in these roles may be required reporters if information about child abuse or neglect comes to them in that capacity.

The statute makes no mention of privileges. The clergy privilege is, apparently, still effective in such proceedings.

[1] N.Y. Civ. Prac. Law sec. 4505 (McKinney 1963 & Supp. 1988).

[2] *In re Wood,* 430 F.Supp. 41 (S.D.N.Y. 1977).

[3] *People v. Shapiro,* 308 N.Y. 150, 141 N.Y.S.2d 562 (1955).

[4] *Kruglikov v. Kruglikov,* 29 Misc.2d 17, 217 N.Y.S.2d 845 (1961), *app. dism'd.,* 16 A.D.2d 735, 226 N.Y.S.2d 931 (1962).

[5] *Keenan v. Gigante,* 64 A.D.2d 585, 407 N.Y.S.2d 163 (1978), *aff'd.,* 47 N.Y.2d 160, 417 N.Y.S.2d 226, 390 N.E.2d 1151 (1979), *cert. denied sub norm. Gigante v. Lankler,* 444 U.S. 887 (1979); *Matter of Fuhrer,* 100 Misc.2d 315, 419 N.Y.S.2d 426 (1979); *People v. Johnson,* 115 A.D.2d 973, 497 N.Y.S.2d 539, *app. denied,* 67 N.Y.2d 885, 501 N.Y.S.2d 1036, 492 N.E.2d 1243 (1985); *People v. Drelich,* 123 A.D.2d 441, 506 N.Y.S.2d 746 (1986).

[6] *Ziske v. Luskin,* 524 N.Y.S.2d 145 (1987).

[7] *De'Udy v. De'Udy,* 130 Misc.2d 168, 495 N.Y.S.2d 616 (1985).

[8] N.Y. Soc. Serv. Law sec. 413 (McKinney 1983 & Supp. 1988).

[9] N.Y. Soc. Serv. Law sec. 414 (McKinney 1983 & Supp. 1988).

NORTH CAROLINA

The statute[1] limits the privilege to a "priest, rabbi, accredited Christian Science practitioner, or a clergyman or ordained minister of an established church." A North Carolina court refused to extend the privilege to a person not an ordained or licensed minister who, nonetheless, had preached and taught Sunday school.[2]

The statute covers "any information which was communicated to him and entrusted to him in his professional capacity, and necessary to enable him to discharge the functions of his office according to the usual course of his practice or discipline, wherein such person so communicating such information about himself or another is seeking spiritual counsel and advice relative to and growing out of the information so imparted." The statute appears to cover all forms of pastoral counseling and has been held to include marriage counseling with both spouses present.[3] Communications not entrusted confidentially to a clergyman, whose wife is present when the communication is made, are not privileged,[4] although if spiritual counsel is sought, the privilege will apply even though the clergyman is a relative.[5]

No clergy "shall be competent to testify" except the privilege "shall not apply where communicant in open court waives the privilege." Consequently, in the face of waiver, the clergyman must testify.

The privilege applies to all actions and proceedings including grand juries.[6]

"Any person or institution who has cause to suspect that any juvenile is abused or neglected shall report the case of that juvenile."[7] There is no exclusion of the clergy as persons required to report.

Although privileges have been abrogated for spouses, physicians and psychologists,[8] the clergy privilege is still effective for proceedings arising out of alleged child abuse.

[1] N.C. Gen. Stat. sec. 8-53.2 (1987 & Supp. 1987).

[2] *State v. Barber,* 317 N.C. 502, 346 S.E.2d 441 (1986).

[3] *Spencer v. Spencer,* 61 N.C.App. 535, 301 S.E.2d 411, *review denied,* 308 N.C. 678, 304 S.E.2d 757 (1983).

[4] *State v. West,* 317 N.C. 219, S.E.2d 186 (1986).

[5] *State v. Jackson,* 77 N.C.App. 832, 336, S.E.2d 437 (1985), *review denied,* 316 N.C. 199, 341 S.E.2d 572 (1986).

[6] N.C. Gen. Stat. sec. 8C-1 Rule 1101 (1987 & Supp. 1987).

[7] N.C. Gen. Stat. sec. 7A-543 (1986 & Supp. 1987).

[8] N.C. Gen. Stat. sec. 7A-551 (1986 & Supp. 1987).

NORTH DAKOTA

The rule of evidence regarding religious privilege[1] defines a clergyman as "a minister, priest, rabbi, accredited Christian Science practitioner, or other similar functionary of a religious organization." It also includes "an individual reasonably believed so to be by the person consulting him." Although no case in North Dakota has further defined the scope of these terms, a court held that the rules of privilege ought to be narrowly construed.[2]

"A communication is confidential if made privately and not intended for further disclosure except to other persons present in furtherance of the purpose of the communication." The privilege is application to "a confidential communication by the person to a clergyman in his professional character as spiritual advisor." The statute appears to include all forms of pastoral counseling within its scope, including marriage counseling with both spouses present.

The privilege may be claimed by the communicant or the clergyman who "is presumed to have the authority to claim the privilege but only on behalf of the communicant." It appears that the clergyman will be compelled to testify in the face of waiver by the communicant.

"The rules with respect to privileges apply at all stages of all actions, cases, and proceedings."[3]

Clergy are not among those required to report under the child abuse reporting statute.[4] However, like others, they may make such a report if they have "reasonable cause to suspect that a child is abused or neglected."

Among required reporters are physicians, mental health professionals, school teachers, administrators or counselors, and social workers. Clergy serving in these roles may be required reporters if information about child abuse or neglect comes to them in that capacity.

The statute[5] abrogates "any privilege of communication between... any professional person and his patient or client, except between attorney and client." It would appear this abrogation includes the clergy privilege.

[1] N.D. R. of Evid. 505 (1974 & Supp. 1987).
[2] *State v. Red Paint,* 311 N.W.2d 182 (N.D. 1981).
[3] N.D. R. of Evid, 1101 (1974 & Supp. 1987).
[4] N.D. Cent. Code sec. 50-25.1-03 (1981 & Supp. 1987).
[5] N.D. Cent. Code sec. 50-25.1-10 (1981 & Supp. 1987).

OHIO

The statute[1] limits the privilege to "a clergyman, rabbi, priest, or regularly ordained, accredited, or licensed minister of an established and legally cognizable church, denomination or sect, when the clergyman... remains accountable to the authority of that church..." No cases have defined the scope of these terms, although it is unlikely the privilege can be constitutionally limited to an established church.

The statute covers "a confession made, or any information confidentially communicated, to him for a religious counseling purpose in his professional character." It appears that pastoral counseling is covered by the privilege, although marriage counseling with both spouses may not be covered. The privilege does not apply to social conversations[2] or to parish census records.[3]

The clergyman "shall not testify" however he "may testify by express consent of the person making the communication, except when the disclosure of the information is in violation of his sacred trust." It is not clear whether a clergyman will be compelled to testify in the fact of waiver by the penitent, however, the seal of confession appears to be protected regardless of waiver.

The privilege is applicable at "all stages of all actions, cases, and proceedings."[4]

Clergy are not among those required to report under the child abuse reporting statute.[5] However, like others, they may make such a report if they have "reason to believe that a child... has suffered... any condition of a nature that reasonably indicates abuse or neglect."

Among required reporters are physicians, licensed psychologists, administrators and employees of child day care centers or child care agencies, school teachers, employees and authorities, and social workers. Clergy serving in these roles may be required reporters if information about child abuse or neglect comes to them in that capacity.

The clergy privilege is not mentioned in the child abuse statute and is apparently effective in proceedings on these matters.

[1]Ohio Rev. Code Ann. sec. 2317.01 (Page 1981 & Supp. 1987).

[2]*In re Soeder's Estate,* 7 Ohio App.2d 271, 220 N.E.2d 547, 36 O.O.2d 404 (1966); *Radecki v. Schuckardt,* 50 Ohio App.2d 92, 361 N.E.2d 543, 4 O.O.3d 60 (1976).

[3]*In re Soeder's Estate,* 7 Ohio App.2d 271, 220 N.E.2d 547, 36 O.O.2d 404 (1966).

[4]Ohio R. of Evid. Rule 101 (Page 1981 & Supp. 1987).

[5]Ohio Rev. Code Ann. sec. 2151.421(A)(1) (Page 1976 & Supp. 1987).

OKLAHOMA

The statute[1] defines a clergyman as "a minister, priest, rabbi, accredited Christian Science practitioner or other similar functionary of a religious organization." It also includes "any individual reasonably believed to be a clergyman by the person consulting him." "Other similar functionary" may provide room for expansion of the privilege to cover a variety of ministries. Although no case in Oklahoma has further defined the scope of these terms, one decision leaves open the question whether a Catholic nun may be considered a clergyman for purposes of the statute.[2]

"A communication is confidential if made privately and not intended for further disclosure except to other persons present in furtherance of the purpose of the communication... A person has a privilege to refuse to disclose and to prevent another from disclosing his confidential communications made to a clergyman acting in his professional capacity." The statute appears to include all forms of pastoral counseling within its scope, including marriage counseling with both spouses present. The privilege does not apply when the clergyman is asked to relay the contents of the communication to a third party.[3]

The privilege may be claimed by the communicant; "the clergyman is presumed to have authority to claim the privilege but only on behalf of the communicant." No case has determined whether the clergyman will be compelled to testify in the face of waiver by the communicant.

The privilege applies "in both criminal and civil proceedings, conducted under the supervision of a court, in which evidence is produced."[4]

The child abuse statute[5] requires "every... person having reason to believe that a child under the age of eighteen years... has had physical injury or injuries inflicted upon him or her by other than accidental means... (to) report the matter promptly." The statute appears to include clergy within its scope.

All privileges, including the clergy privilege, have been abrogated in matters regarding child abuse.[6]

[1]Okla. Stat. Ann. tit. 12, sec. 2505 (West 1980 & Supp. 1988).
[2]*Masquat v. Maguire,* 638 P.2d 1105 (Okla. 1981).
[3]*Naum v. State,* 630 P.2d 785 (Okla. Crim. 1981), *cert. denied,* 454 U.S. 1058 (1981).
[4]Okla. Stat. Ann. tit. 12, sec. 2103(a) (West 1980 & Supp. 1988).
[5]Okla. Stat. Ann. tit. 21, sec. 846 (West 1983 & Supp. 1988).
[6]Okla. Stat. Ann. tit. 21, sec. 848 (West 1983 & Supp. 1988).

OREGON

The statute[1] defines a "member of the clergy" as "a minister of any church, religious denomination or organization or accredited Christian Science practitioner who in the course of the discipline or practice of that church... is authorized or accustomed to hearing confidential communications and, under the discipline or tenets of that church... has a duty to keep such communications secret." An Oregon court has included the stake president of the Mormon Church within this definition.[2]

The statute covers "a communication made privately and not intended for further disclosure except to other persons present in furtherance of the purpose of the communication" and "made to the member of the clergy in the member's professional character." The statute appears to include all forms of pastoral counseling within its scope including marriage counseling with both spouses present.

The clergyman cannot be examined "without the consent of the person making the communication." No case has determined whether the clergyman will be compelled to testify if the communicant gives his consent.

The privilege applies "at all stages of all actions, suits and proceedings.[3]

Clergy are required reporters under the child abuse reporting statute.[4] However, the clergy "shall not be required to report such information communicated by a person if the communication is privileged."[5]

Other required reporters include physicians, school employees, psychologists, and social workers. Clergy serving in these roles may be required reporters if information about child abuse or neglect comes to them in that capacity.

The privileges for spouses, psychotherapists, physicians, social workers, and staff members of schools have been abrogated in matters regarding child abuse. The clergy privilege is apparently still effective.

[1]Or. Rev. Stat. sec. 40.260 Rule 506 (1987).
[2]*State v. Cox,* 87 Or. App. 443, 742 P.2d 694 (1986).
[3]Or. Rev. Stat. sec. 40.015 Rule 101(3) (1987).
[4]Or. Rev. Stat. sec. 418.750 and sec. 418.740(3)(h) (1987).
[5]Or. Rev. Stat. sec. 418.740(3)(h) (1987).

PENNSYLVANIA

The statute[1] limits the privilege to a "clergyman, priest, rabbi or minister of the gospel of any regularly established church or religious organization, except clergymen or ministers who are self-ordained or who are members of religious organizations in which members other than the leader thereof are deemed clergymen or ministers." No case has defined the scope of these terms, although it is unlikely the privilege can be constitutionally limited to an established church.

The statute covers communications made to a clergyman, "who while in the course of his duties has acquired information from any person secretly and in confidence." The statute is to be strictly construed[2] and statements not made in confidence[3] or not of a penitential character[4] are not privileged; clergymen may testify to matters which are not confidential.[5] The statute includes all forms of pastoral counseling as well as individual marriage counseling.[6] The presence of two ministers does not break the privilege.[7]

No clergyman "shall be compelled or allowed (to testify) without consent of such person." No case has determined whether the clergyman will be compelled to testify if the communicant gives his consent.

The privilege is applicable "in any legal proceeding, trial or investigation before any government unit." It is error to put the clergyman on the witness stand knowing he will invoke the privilege.[8]

The child protective service statute[9] requires "any person who, in the course of their employment, occupation, or practice of their profession come(s) into contact with children, shall report... when they have reason to believe, on the basis of their medical, professional or other training and experience, that a child coming before them in their professional or official capacity is an abused child." The statute appears to include the clergy within its scope.

The clergy privilege has been retained for child abuse proceedings.[10]

[1] Pa. Cons. Stat. Ann. tit. 42, sec. 5943 (Purdon 1981 & Supp. 1988).

[2] *LeGore v. LeGore*, 31 Pa. D. & C.2d 107 (1963).

[3] *In re McGrogan's Will*, 26 Pa.D. & C.2d 37 (1961); *Fahlfeder c. Commonwealth, Pennsylvania Bd. of Probation and Parole*, 80 Pa. Cmwlth, 86, 470 A.2d 1130.

[4] *In re Shaeffer's Estate*, 52 Dauph. 45 (Pa. County Ct. 1942).

[5] *Commonwealth ex rel. M.B. v. L.D.B.*, 295 Pa. Super. 1, 440 A.2d 1192 (1982).

[6] *LeGore v. LeGore*, 31 Pa. D. & C.2d 1192 (1982).

[7] *Commonwealth v. Shallenberger*, 38 Pa. D. & C.3d 201 (1985).

[8] *Commonwealth v. Musolini*, 320 Pa. Super. 425, 456 A.2d 605 (1983).

[9] Pa. Stat. Ann. tit. 11, sec. 2207 (Purdon 1965 & Supp. 1988).

[10] Pa. Stat. Ann. tit. 11, sec. 2222 (Purdon 1965 & Supp. 1988).

RHODE ISLAND

The statute[1] limits the privilege to "clergymen or priest... minister of the gospel... or rabbi." No case has defined the scope of these terms.

The statute covers "any confession made to him in his professional character in the course of discipline enjoined by the church to which he belongs." It also covers "any confidential communication, properly entrusted to him in his professional capacity, and necessary and proper to enable him to discharge the functions of his office in the usual course of practice or discipline." The statute appears to include all forms of pastoral counseling within its scope, although marriage counseling with both spouses present may not be included.

"No clergyman... shall be compelled to testify... without the consent of the person making the confession... (or) communication." No case has determind whether the clergyman will be compelled to testify if the communicant gives his consent.

The privilege is applicable "in the trial of every cause, both civil and criminal."

"Any person who has reasonable cause to know or suspect that any child has been abused or neglected... shall, within twenty-four hours, transfer such information to the department for children and their families."[2] "Any person... who has reasonable cause to know or suspect that a child has died as a result of child abuse or neglect shall immediately transfer such information to the department.[3] The statute apparently includes clergy within its scope.

"The privileged quality of communication between husband and wife and any professional person and his patient or client, except that between attorney and client, is... abrogated in situations involving known or suspected child abuse or neglect and shall not constitute grounds for failure to report as required... failure to cooperate with the department... or failure to give or accept evidence in any judicial proceeding.[4]

[1]R.I. Gen. Laws sec. 9-17-23 (1985 & Supp. 1987).
[2]R.I. Gen. Laws sec. 40-11-3 (1984 & Supp. 1987).
[3]R.I. Gen. Laws sec. 40-11-3.1 (1984 & Supp. 1987).
[4]R.I. Gen. Laws sec. 40-11-11 (1984 & Supp. 1987).

SOUTH CAROLINA

The statute[1] limits the privilege to a "regular or duly ordained minister, priest or rabbi." No case has defined the scope of these terms.

The statute covers "any confidential communication properly entrusted to him in his professional capacity and necessary and proper to enable him to discharge the functions of his office according to the usual course of practice or discipline of his church or religious body." The statute appears to include all forms of pastoral counseling within its scope and has been held to include marriage counseling.[2] The court has left open the extent to which a clergyman's records are protected.[3]

No clergyman "shall be required in giving testimony, to disclose any confidential communication." However, the "prohibition shall not apply to cases where the party in whose favor it is made waives the rights conferred." A clergyman may be compelled to testify in face of waiver by the communicant.

The privilege applies "in any legal or quasi-legal trial, hearing or proceeding before any court, commission or committee" and the application is within the discretion of the judge.[4]

Clergy are not among those required to report under the child abuse reporting statute.[5] However, like others, they may make such a report if they have "reason to believe that a child's physical or mental health or welfare has been or may be adversely affected by abuse and neglect."

Among required reporters are physicians, mental health professionals, school teachers and counselors, and social workers. Clergy serving in these roles may be required reporters if information about child abuse or neglect comes to them in that capacity.

Although most privileges have been abrogated in matters involving child abuse, the clergy privilege has been retained.[6]

[1]S.C. Code Ann. sec. 19-11-90 (Law. Co-op. 1985 & Supp. 1987).
[2]*Rivers v. Rivers,* 292 S.C. 21, 354 S.E.2d 784 (1987).
[3]*State v. Franklin,* 267 S.C. 240, 226 S.E.2d 896 (1976).
[4]*Id.*
[5]S.C. Code Ann. sec. 20-7-510 (Law Co-op. 1985 & Supp. 1987).
[6]S.C. Code Ann. sec. 20-7-550 (Law Co-op. 1985 & Supp. 1987).

SOUTH DAKOTA

The statute[1] limits the privilege to "a minister, priest, rabbi, acredited Christian Science practitioner, or other similar functionary of a religious organization." It also includes "an individual reasonably believed so to be by the person consulting him." "Other similar functionary" may provide room for expansion of the privilege to cover a variety of ministries, however, no case has defined the scope of these terms.

"A communication is confidential if made privately and not intended for further disclosure except to other persons present in furtherance of the purpose of the communication."[2] The privilege is applicable to confidential communications made "by the person to a clergyman in his professional capacity as a spiritual advisor."[3] The statute appears to include all forms of pastoral counseling within its scope, including marriage counseling with both spouses present.

The privilege may be claimed by the communicant or by "the person who was the clergyman at the time of the communication (and who) is presumed to have authority to claim the privilege but only on behalf of the communicant."[4]

The privilege applies to actions and proceedings in court.[5]

Clergy are not among those required to report under the child abuse reporting statute.[6] However, like others, a clergyman may make a report if he "knows, suspects, or has reason to believe that a child has received physical or emotional injury or injuries as the result of abuse or intentional neglect."

Among required reporters are physicians; mental health professionals; social workers; school teachers, counselors, and officials; and licensed child welfare providers. Clergy serving in these roles may be required

[1]S.D. Codified Laws Ann. sec. 19-13-16(1) (1987 & Supp. 1988).
[2]S.D. Codified Laws Ann. sec. 19-13-16(2) (1987 & Supp. 1988).
[3]S.D. Codified Laws Ann. sec. 19-13-17 (1987 & Supp. 1988).
[4]S.D. Codified Laws Ann. sec. 19-13-18 (1987 & Supp. 1988).
[5]S.D. Codified Laws Ann. sec. 19-9-14 (1987 & Supp. 1988).
[6]S.D. Codified Laws Ann. sec. 26-10-10 (1984 & Supp. 1988).

reporters if information about child abuse or neglect comes to them in that capacity.

Although most privileges have been abrogated, the clergy privilege is effective for child abuse proceedings.[7]

[7]S.D. Codified Laws Ann. sec. 26-10-15 (1984 & Supp. 1988).

TENNESSEE

The statute[1] limits the privilege to a "minister of the gospel, ... priest of the Catholic Church, ... ordained rabbi, and ... regular minister of any religious organization or denomination usually referred to as a church, over the age of eighteen years." No case has defined the scope of these terms.

The statute covers "any information communicated to him in a confidential manner, properly entrusted to him in his professional capacity, and necessary to enable him to discharge the functions of his office according to the usual course of his practice or discipline, wherein such person so communicating such information about himself or another is seeking spiritual counsel and advice relative to and growing out of the information so imparted." The statute appears to cover all forms of pastoral counseling, though marriage counseling with both spouses present may not be included.

A clergyman shall not be allowed or required to give testimony as a witness in litigation, however, the privilege "shall not apply to cases where the communicating party, or parties, waives the right so conferred by personal appearance in open court ... or by an affidavit." No case has determined whether a clergyman will be compelled to testify in face of waiver by the communicant, however, the statute contains fine and imprisonment penalties for "violating the provisions" of this statute.

The privilege is applicable for "any litigation" and the trial judge has discretion to determine the qualifications of the clergyman.

"Any person ... having knowledge of or called upon to render aid to any child from ... (a) condition which is of such a nature as to reasonably indicate that it has been caused by brutality, abuse or neglect ... shall report such harm immediately."[2] The statute appears to include clergy within its scope.

The privileges for spouses, psychiatrists, and psychologists have been abrogated in matters regarding child abuse, however, the clergy privilege is apparently effective in these proceedings.

[1]Tenn. Code Ann. sec. 24-1-206 (1980 & Supp. 1987).
[2]Tenn. Code Ann. sec. 37-1-403 (1984 & Supp. 1987).

TEXAS

Texas has separate rules of evidence for civil[1] and criminal[2] cases. The clergy privilege rule is identical in each.

The rules define a clergyman as "a minister, priest, rabbi, accredited Christian Science practitioner, or other similar functionary of a religious organization." It also includes "an individual reasonably believed so to be by the person consulting him." "Other similar functionary" may provide room for expansion of the privilege to cover a variety of ministries, however, no case has defined the scope of these terms.

"A communication is confidential if made privately and not intended for further disclosure except to other persons present in furtherance of the purpose of the communication." The privilege is applicable to "a confidential communication by the person to a clergyman in his professional character as spiritual advisor." The statute appears to include all forms of pastoral counseling within its scope, including marriage counseling with both spouses present.

The privilege may be claimed by the communicant or "the person who was the clergyman at the time of the communication... but only on behalf of the communicant." It appears that the clergyman will be compelled to testify in the face of waiver by the communicant.

The privilege is applicable in civil and criminal proceedings.[3]

"Any person having cause to believe that a child's physical or mental health or welfare has been or may be adversely affected by abuse or neglect by a person responsible for the child's care, custody or welfare shall (make a) report."[4] The Texas Attorney General has ruled that "clergymen are covered by this section."[5]

The statute has abrogated all privileges in child abuse matters except attorney-client privilege.[6]

[1]Tex. R. of Civ. Evid., Rule 505 (West 1987).
[2]Tex. R. of Crim. Evid., Rule 505 (West 1987).
[3]Tex. R. of Civ. Evid., Rule 101 (West 1987); Tex. R. of Crim. Evid., Rule 101 (West 1987).
[4]Tex. Fam. Code Ann. sec. 34.01 (Vernon 1986 & Supp. 1988).
[5]Op. Tex. Att'y. Gen. No. JM-342 (1985).
[6]Tex. Fam. Code Ann. sec. 34.04 (Vernon 1986 & Supp. 1988).

UTAH

The statute[1] limits the privilege to "a clergyman or priest." No case has defined the scope of these terms.

The statute covers "any confession made to him in his professional character in the course of discipline enjoined by the church to which he belongs." Because the statute is limited to confessions, other kinds of communication, such as pastoral counseling, may not be covered. No case has determined the extent of the communications covered.

The clergyman cannot be examined "without the consent of the person making the confession." No case has determined whether the clergyman will be compelled to testify if the communicant gives his consent.

The privilege is applicable in all actions where a person may be examined as a witness.

Although any person who has reason to believe a child has been abused or neglected is a required reporter under the child abuse reporting act,[2] the act also contains an exception for the clergy. "The notification requirements... do not apply to a clergyman or priest, without the consent of the person making the confession, with regard to any confession made to him in his professional character in the course of discipline enjoined by the church to which he belongs, if: (a) the confession was made directly to the clergyman or priest by the perpetrator; and (b) the clergyman or priest is, under canon law or church doctrine or practice, bound to maintain the confidentiality of that confession."[3]

The statute further requires that "if a clergyman or priest receives information about abuse or neglect from any source other than the confession of the perpetrator, he is required to give notification on the basis of that information even though he may have also received a report of abuse or neglect from the confession of the perpetrator. Exemption of notification requirements for a clergyman or priest does not exempt a clergyman or priest from any other efforts required by law to prevent further abuse or neglect by the perpetrator."[4]

The statute has abrogated the physician privilege in child abuse matters,[5] however the clergy privilege is apparently effective in these matters.

[1]Utah Code Ann. sec. 78-24-8(3) (1987 & Supp. 1988).
[2]Utah Code Ann. sec. 62A-4-503(1) (1986 & Supp. 1988).
[3]Utah Code Ann. sec. 62A-4-503(2) (1986 & Supp. 1988).
[4]Utah Code Ann. sec. 62A-4-503(3) (1986 & Supp. 1988).
[5]Utah Code Ann. sec. 62A-4-513(4) (1986 & Supp. 1988).

VERMONT

The rule of evidence regarding religious privilege[1] defines a clergyman as "a minister, priest, rabbi, accredited Christian Science practitioner, or other similar functionary of a religious organization." It also includes "an individual reasonably believed so to be by the person consulting him." "Other similar functionary" may provide room for expansion of the rule to cover a variety of ministries, however, no case has defined the scope of these terms.

"A communication is confidential if made privately and not intended for further disclosure except to other persons present in furtherance of the purposes of the communication." The privilege is applicable to confidential communications made "by the person to a clergyman in his professional character as a spiritual advisor." The statute appears to include all forms of pastoral counseling within its scope, including marriage counseling with both spouses present. A court has held a priest's refusal to testify to the identity of a person providing cash bail for a defendant arrested for arson falls within the privilege.[2]

The privilege may be claimed by the communicant or by the clergyman who "is presumed to have authority to claim the privilege, but only on behalf of the communicant." No case has determined whether the clergyman will be compelled to testify in face of waiver by the communicant.

The privilege applies in "all actions and proceedings in the courts" including those before grand juries.[3]

Clergy are not among those required to report under the child abuse reporting statute.[4] However, like others, they may make such a report if they have "reasonable cause to believe that any child has been abused or neglected."

Among required reporters are physicians, psychologists, school teachers and guidance counselors, mental health professionals, and social workers. Clergy serving in these roles may be required reporters if information about child abuse or neglect comes to them in that capacity.

The clergy privilege is not mentioned in the child abuse statute and is apparently effective in these proceedings.

[1]Vt. R. of Evid. 505 (1983 & Supp. 1987).
[2]*State v. Bonilla,* Dist. Ct., Rutland Cir., No. 1132-7-84 Rcr (Feb. 4, 1985).
[3]Vt. R. of Evid. 1101 (1983 & Supp. 1987).
[4]Vt. Stat. Ann. tit. 33, sec. 683 (1981 & Supp. 1987).

VIRGINIA

The statute[1] limits the privilege to a "regular minister, priest, rabbi or accredited practitioner over the age of eighteen years, of any religious organization or denomination usually referred to as a church." No case has defined the scope of these terms.

The statute covers "any information communicated to him in a confidential manner, properly entrusted to him in his professional capacity and necessary to enable him to discharge the functions of his office according to the usual course of his practice or discipline, wherein such person so communicating such information about himself or another is seeking spiritual counsel and advice relative to and growing out of the information so imparted." It appears that pastoral counseling is covered by the privilege, although marriage counseling with both spouses present may not be covered.

No clergyman "shall be required... to disclose any information." The federal court applying Virginia law decided that the privilege is the clergyman's alone to claim and cannot be affected by the communicant.[2]

The privilege is applicable "in giving testimony as a witness in any civil action."

Clergy are not among those required to report under the child abuse reporting statute.[3] However, like others, a clergyman may make such a report if he "suspects that a child is an abused or neglected child."

Among required reporters are persons licensed to practice medicine, social workers, teachers or other employees of a private or public school, kindergarten or nursery school, and mental health professionals. A Virginia court has held the reporting requirement applicable to church-run child care centers.[4] Clergy serving in these roles may be required reporters if information about child abuse or neglect comes to them in that capacity.

Although privileges have been abrogated for spouses and physicians,[5] the clergy privilege is apparently effective in these proceedings.

[1]Va. Code Ann. sec. 8.01-400 (1984 & Supp. 1988).

[2]*Seidman v. Fishburne-Hudgins Educational Foundation, Inc.*, 724 F.2d 413 (4th Cir. 1984).

[3]Va. Code Ann. sec. 63.1-248.3 (1987 & Supp. 1988).

[4]*Forest Hills Early Learning Center, Inc. v. Lukhard,* 661 F. Supp. 300 (E.D. Va. 1987).

[5]Va. Code Ann. sec. 63-1-248.11 (1987 & Supp. 1988).

WASHINGTON

The statute[1] limits the privilege to a "member of the clergy or a priest." No case has defined the scope of these terms.

The statute covers "any confession made to him or her in his or her professional character, in the course of discipline enjoined by the church to which he or she belongs." Because the statute is limited to confessions, other kinds of communication, such as pastoral counseling may not be covered.

The clergyman cannot be examined "without the consent of a person making the confession." No case has determined whether the clergyman will be compelled to testify if the communicant gives his consent.

The privilege applies in all judicial proceedings.

The abuse and neglect reporting statute applies to children and adult dependent or developmentally disabled persons. Clergy are not among those required to report under the statute.[2] However, like others, they may make such a report if they have "reasonable cause to believe that a child or adult dependent or developmentally disabled person has suffered abuse or neglect." The statute also states that "conduct conforming with the reporting requirements... shall not be deemed a violation of the confidential communication privilege of (clergymen)."[3]

Among required reporters are physicians; school teachers, counselors, and administrators; social service counselors; and psychologists. Clergy serving in these roles may be required reporters if information about child abuse or neglect comes to them in that capacity.

The clergy privilege, except as above, is not mentioned in the abuse and neglect statute and is apparently effective in these proceedings.

[1] Wash. Rev. Code Ann. sec. 5.60.060(3) (1963 & Supp. 1988).
[2] Wash. Rev. Code Ann. sec. 26.44.030 (1986 & Supp. 1988).
[3] Wash. Rev. Code Ann. sec. 26.44.060(3) (1986 & Supp. 1988).

WEST VIRGINIA

The statute[1] limits the privilege to a "priest, minister, rabbi or other clergyman... of any religious denomination or organization." No case has defined the scope of these terms.

The statute covers "any communications or statements made to such clergyman in his capacity as spiritual counselor or spiritual advisor... if (a) both the clergyman and the party making such communications or statements claim that the communications or statements were made to the clergyman in his capacity as a clergyman and spiritual counselor or spiritual advisor to such party; and (b) no person, other than the clergyman, such party and the spouse of such party, was present when such communications or statements were made." The statute appears to include all forms of pastoral counseling within its scope, including marriage counseling with both spouses present.

Clergymen cannot be compelled to testify if "the party making such communications or statements does not either consent to their disclosure or otherwise waive the privilge." No case has determined whether the clergyman will be compelled to testify in the face of waiver by the communicant.

The privilege applies only to actions brought under the divorce and annulment statute.

Clergy are not among those required to report under the child abuse reporting statute.[2] However, like others, they may make such a report if they have "reasonable cause to suspect that a child has been abused or neglected."

Among required reporters are physicians, mental health professionals, school teachers and other personnel, and social service workers. Clergy serving in these roles may be required reporters if information about child abuse or neglect comes to them in that capacity.

The statute[3] abrogates "the privileged quality of communications between... any professional person and his patient or client, except that between attorney and client." It would appear this abrogation includes the clergy privilege.

[1] W. Va. Code sec. 48-2-10a (1986 & Supp. 1988).
[2] W. Va. Code sec. 49-6A-2 (1986 & Supp. 1988).
[3] W. Va. Code sec. 49-6A-7 (1986 & Supp. 1988).

WISCONSIN

The statute[1] defines a clergyman as "a minister, priest, rabbi, or other similar functionary of a religious organization." It also includes "an individual reasonably believed so to be by the person consulting him." "Other similar functionary" may provide room for expansion of the privilege to cover a variety of ministries, however, no case has defined the scope of these terms.

"A communication is confidential if made privately and not intended for further disclosure except to other persons present in furtherance of the purpose of the communication." The privilege is applicable to "a confidential communication by the person to a clergyman in his professional character as a spiritual advisor." The statute appears to include all forms of pastoral counseling within its scope, including marriage counseling with both spouses present. The privilege does not apply when the communication is not made to the clergyman in his professional character.[2]

The privilege may be claimed by the communicant or by the clergyman on behalf of the person and "his authority so to do is presumed in the absence of evidence to the contrary." No case has determined whether the clergyman will be compelled to testify in face of waiver by the communicant.

The privilege is applicable "at all stages of all actions, cases and proceedings."[3] A court held the privilege inapplicable to out-of-control disclosures, for example, during the course of a police interrogation where the disclosure of a privileged communication was used as a source of acquiring evidence.[4]

Clergy are not among those required to report under the child abuse reporting statute.[5] However, like others, they may make such a report if they have "reason to suspect that a child has been abused or neglected or reason to believe that a child has been threatened with abuse or neglect."

Among required reporters are physicians; mental health professionals; social workers; school teachers, administrators and counselors; and day care providers. Clergy serving in these roles may be required reporters if information about child abuse or neglect comes to them in that capacity.

The clergy privilege is not mentioned in the child abuse statute and is apparently effective in these proceedings.

[1]Wis. Stat. Ann. sec. 905.06 (West 1975 & Supp. 1987).

[2]*Colbert v. State,* 125 Wis. 423, 104 N.W. 61 (1905).

[3]Wis. Stat. Ann. sec. 911.01(3) (West 1975 & Supp. 1987).

[4]*State v. Kunkel,* 137 Wis. 2d 172, 404 N.W.2d 69, *review denied,* 138 Wis. 2d 531, 412 N.W.2d 893, *cert. denied,* 108 S.Ct. 297 (1987).

[5]Wis. Stat. Ann. sec. 48.981(2) (1987 & Supp. 1987).

WYOMING

The statute[1] limits the privilege to "a clergyman or priest." No case has defined the scope of these terms.

The statute covers "a confession made to him in his professional character if enjoined by the church to which he belongs." Because the statute is limited to confessions, other kinds of communication, such as pastoral counseling, may not be covered.

Since the statute states clergyman "shall not testify," waiver by the communicant will not destroy the privilege.

The privilege applies in all judicial proceedings.

The child abuse statute[2] requires "any person who knows or has reasonable cause to believe or suspect that a child has been abused or neglected ... (to) immediately report it." The statute appears to include clergy within its scope.

The clergy privilege has been retained in judicial proceedings resulting from such reports of alleged abuse.[3]

[1]Wyo. Stat. Ann. sec. 1-12-101(a)(ii) (1988 & Supp. 1988).

[2]Wyo. Stat. Ann. sec. 14-3-205(a) (1986 & Supp. 1988).

[3]Wyo. Stat. Ann. sec. 14-3-210(1)(ii) (1986 & Supp. 1988).

The Canonical Tradition of Confidentiality Pertaining to Oral Communications

MARIE BREITENBECK, O.P.

Overview of the 1983 Code of Canon Law

In addressing the concept of confidentiality in transmission of the spoken word, the most obvious example of such confidentiality within canon law is the seal of confession, which is governed by canon 1388, §§1, 2 of Book VI, "Sanctions in the Church", and by canons 983, §§1, 2 and 984, §§1, 2 of Book IV, "The Office of Sanctifying in the Church". Canons 1130-1133 governing confidentiality concerning marriages secretly celebrated are also found in Book IV. In addition to the canons found in these two books, canons governing confidentiality of oral communications are found in three other books of the revised code, namely, Book I, "General Norms" (c. 127, §3); Book II, "The People of God" (cc. 377, §§2, 3; 471, nn. 1,2; 645, §4); and Book VII, "Processes" (cc. 1455, §§1, 2, 3; 1457, §§1, 2; 1548, §2, n.1; 1602, §1; 1609, §3). In addition to those canons which specifically legislate confidentiality of oral communications there are other canons which could include some dimension of confidentiality regarding oral communication, such as: canon 220, which protects a person's good reputation and a person's right to privacy; canon 630, §5 which exhorts members of religious communities to approach superiors with trust; canon 642 regarding admittance of members to a religious institute; and canons 1656-1670, which govern the oral contentious process.

Confessional Secrecy

Since the most obvious example of oral confidentiality is found in legislation pertinent to the seal of confession and to secrecy in matters of sacramental confession those canons will be addressed first, followed by canons presented in the other books of the Code according to the order established by the Commission for the Revision of Canon Law.

Current church law clearly articulates the well-established historical-canonical tradition[1] governing secrecy regarding matters spoken of in sacramental confession.

> The sacramental seal is inviolable; therefore, it is a crime for a confessor in any way to betray a penitent by word or in any other manner or for any reason.
>
> An interpreter, if there is one, is also obliged to preserve the secret and also all others to whom knowledge of sins from confession shall come in any way.[2]

The 1917 *Code of Canon Law* likewise obliged to secrecy the confessor, interpreter, and any others privy to confessional matters.[3] However, the language of canon 889, §1 of the former Code governing the responsibility of the confessor was not as strongly worded as the current canon in that the former Code stated that the confessor was "carefully to guard against" betraying the penitent by words or signs or in any way or for any reason. Likewise, the Rite of Penance, revised following the Second Vatican Council and issued prior to the promulgation of the revised Code,[4] while honoring the traditional language of secrecy, is not as strongly worded as the revised Code.

> As the minister of God the confessor comes to know the secrets of another's conscience, and he is bound to keep the sacramental seal of confession absolutely inviolable.[5]

[1] See Bertrand Kurtscheid, *A History of the Seal of Confession,* trans. F.A. Marks, (St. Louis, MO: B. Herder Book Co., 1927). Kurtscheid traces the history of the secrecy of the seal of confession to legislation of Leo I in 459, observing that such legislation was universally accentuated during the Middle Ages, accompanied by the teaching that the secrecy of the seal obligates under divine law. He traces penal legislation for violation of the seal to the close of the ninth century. During the Middle Ages he notes that, due to the fact that principles of canon law concerning the seal of confession were sanctioned by civil governments, violation of the seal was, in turn, severely punished by secular judges.

[2] c. 983, §§1,2. Canon 990 permitted the use of interpreters. Unless otherwise indicated, canon numbers refer to the 1983 *Code of Canon Law.*

[3] 1917 CIC: c. 889, §§1,2. Canon 903 of the 1917 Code permitted the use of interpreters.

[4] Sacra Congregatio pro Cultu Divino, decree *Ordo Paenitentiae,* December 2, 1973: Typis Polyglottis Vaticanis, 1974. Translation in International Commission on English in the Liturgy (Hereafter cited ICEL). *The Rites of the Catholic Church* (New York: Pueblo Publishing Co., 1976), pp. 339-406.

[5] *Ordo Paenitentiae,* n. 10d: *The Rites of the Catholic Church,* p. 349.

Thomas J. Green observes that the reformulated version found in the revised Code is written to speak of the confessor doing wrong in breaking the secrecy of the confessional seal rather than being obliged to maintain it as in the original canon of both the old Code and the 1980 *Schema.*[6] Frederick McManus states that the revised Code uses the words "it is a crime" rather than repeat the old Code wording of "carefully guard against," for the specific purpose of stressing the gravity of the violation of the norm of secrecy.[7] What is common to both Green and McManus as well as to the authors of both Codes and of the revised Rite of Penance, is concern that confidentiality be preserved by the minister of the sacrament as well as any other persons privy to knowledge received through the celebration of the sacrament. In both Codes the obligation to observe and preserve such confidentiality binds each and every recipient in all matters learned through confession of sins by a penitent. Each Code expresses this concern for confidentiality regarding confessional matters somewhat differently. The 1917 Code stated that it was the sacramental seal itself which bound the confessor, the interpreter, and anyone who was privy to confessional matter. The revised Code distinguishes between the seal of confession which binds the confessor and makes it a crime for him to betray a penitent, and an obligation to preserve secrecy which binds an interpreter and others privy to confessional matters. As can be seen from the legislation of both Codes, neither expression weakens the seriousness of the obligation to secrecy. The obligation, by whatever name, is serious and binds *all* recipients of sacramental matters. Neither code permits exceptions to the norms of the respective canons. The all encompassing nature of confidentiality as it pertains to confessional matters, is articulated clearly by McManus.

[6]Thomas J. Green, "Final Changes in the Revised Code of Canon Law," p. 15. This unpublished text is a list indicating those changes in the revised code, which had been made since the 1980 *Schema* was published. The wording of canon 889, §1 of the 1917 Code and that of canon 937, §1 of the 1980 *Schema* is very similar and of different emphasis than canon 983, §1 of the revised Code.

[7]Frederick R. McManus, "Title IV: The Sacrament of Penance (cc. 959-997)," in *The Code of Canon Law: A Text and Commentary,* ed. James A. Coriden et al. (New York/Mahwah: Paulist Press, 1985) (Hereafter called *Commentary*), p. 691.

> ...No distinction is made among the matters confessed, whether the sinful action itself or attendant circumstances, or the acts of satisfaction or penalties imposed, etc. The secrecy concerning the penitent and his or her confession of sins that is to be maintained is properly described as total.[8]

Having legislated secrecy regarding confessional matter as it pertains to all persons privy to such information, the law focuses specifically upon the confessor.

> Even if every danger of revelation is excluded, a confessor is absolutely forbidden to use knowledge acquired from confession when it might harm the penitent.
>
> One who is placed in authority can in no way use for external governance knowledge about sins which he has received in confession at any time.[9]

This canon is not new to the revised Code. Rather, the basic tenets and restrictions of the canon were found in the previous Code.[10] McManus observes that the twofold concern of this canon is with any other use of knowledge obtained in the course of individual celebration of the sacrament, even when there is no disclosure of a person's sins.[11] According to McManus, the sense of the first paragraph of the canon is that the confessor may become aware of incidental information in the course of confession. Such information, however, may not be used or disclosed in any way that may be hurtful or detrimental to the penitent, or that in any way reveals the identity of the penitent.[12] An instruction of the Holy Office, issued in 1915, strongly affirmed the importance of secrecy regarding matters learned in confession by counseling avoidance of all talk and any references to such matters, whether references be through preaching, instructions, or in private conversation.[13] At the time the instruc-

[8]McManus, *Commentary,* p. 691.

[9]c. 984, §§1,2.

[10]1917 CIC: c. 890, §§1,2.

[11]McManus, p. 692.

[12]Ibid., at 691-692.

[13]Suprema Sacra Congregazione del Santo Ufficio, instructio *ad Rev. mos locorum Ordinarios familiarumque religiosarum Moderatores super inviolabili sanctitate sigilli sacramentalis,* June 9, 1915: *Il Monitor Ecclesiatico* 29 (1917) 199-201, at 200. See also Stanislaus Woywod and Callistus Smith, *A Practical Commentary on the Code of Canon Law* (New York: Joseph F. Wagner, Inc., 1943), 1: 435-436.

tion was issued the Holy Office indicated the purpose of such an instruction was to explain the full impact of the divine law which bound the confessor to absolute secrecy regarding what was heard in sacramental confession. Therefore, it would seem that the strong exhortation regarding the importance of maintaining secrecy is no less binding today than it was in 1915.[14]

The second paragraph of canon 984 prohibits anyone in a position of authority from using for external governance any knowledge about sins which such person has received in confession at any time. This section of the canon is similar to its 1917 predecessor.[15] Both the 1917 Code and the revised Code clearly reflect the ongoing tradition of secrecy regarding confessional matters in prohibiting all authority figures from utilizing in their external governance, any material received in sacramental confession.

Further proof of the seriousness with which church law regards oral confidentiality within the context of the sacrament of penance is found in canon 1388:

> A confessor who directly violates the seal of confession incurs an automatic *(latae sententiae)* excommunication reserved to the Apostolic See; if he does so only indirectly, he is to be punished in accord with the seriousness of the offense.
>
> An interpreter and other persons mentioned in c. 983, §2, who violate this secrecy are to be punished with a just penalty not excluding excommunication.[16]

[14]Both the Commentary of the Canon Law Society of America (p. 692) and the Spanish Commentary from Pamplona (Pedro Lombardia y Juan Ignacio Arrieta, eds., *Codigo de Derecho Canonico,* edicion anotada (EUNSA, 1983)), pp. 593-594 refer to this 1915 instruction regarding the importance of secrecy concerning any knowledge learned from sacramental confession in their commentaries on canon 984, §1 of the present Code.

[15]1917 CIC: c. 890, §2.

[16]H.A. Ayrinhac (*Penal Legislation in the New Code of Canon Law,* revised by P.J. Lydon (New York: Benziger Brothers, 1936), p. 277) states that the seal of confession is violated: 1) directly when any matter of the seal is explicitly disclosed and the person of the penitent clearly designated, whether that person be known to the hearers or not, whether they realize or not that the information conveyed to them was obtained through sacramental confession; 2) indirectly when the revelation is not intended but permitted, i.e., there is danger that the person will be known or that suspicion of a person's sin may result. In a wide sense there is indirect violation when there is no danger of revealing any one's sin but the act of the priest renders the confession odious, e.g., if the confessor in private changes his attitude towards the penitent outside of confession and becomes cold, etc. towards the person. See also John R. Roos, *The Seal of Confession,* Canon Law Studies, 413 (Washington: The Catholic University of America, 1960), pp. 79-82.

The first paragraph of the canon closely reflects canon 2369, §1 of the 1917 Code in reiterating the seriousness of the confessor's obligation to preserve the seal of confession. While the language of the 1917 Code did not indicate specifically that the confessor incurred automatic, that is *latae sententiae*, excommunication as does the present code, Woywod and Smith stated that they, as well as other commentators on the 1917 Code, almost unanimously taught that the excommunication was incurred automatically since the 1917 Code made the censure involved reserved to the Apostolic See, and reservation of *ferendae sententiae* penalties was foreign to ecclesiastical court procedure.[17] Furthermore, communiques from the Congregation for the Doctrine of the Faith, which specifically addressed abuses of the sacredness of confession, declared that those who violated secrecy concerning confessional matters incurred a *latae sententiae* excommunication, namely: 1) persons seeking to profane the sacrament of penance and violate its secrecy, whether that be done by making "a tape or recording of sacramental confessions, whether genuine or feigned, by use of any kind of mechanical device, or publishing confessions obtained in this manner;"[18] 2) persons giving formal cooperation to such or similar publications, whether as author or collaborator;[19] and, 3) persons taking part in advertising or distributing the publication.[20]

Interestingly, the whole notion of the penalty of excommunication for direct violation of the seal of confession by a confessor, as indicated in the 1917 Code, was not repeated in the 1980 *Schema*[21] nor does the 1981 *Relatio* record any discussion either of reservation of this penalty to the Apostolic See, or of such a penalty being a *latae sententiae* penalty.[22] However, when the

[17]Woywod-Smith 2: 510.

[18]Sacra Congregatio pro Doctrina Fidei, declaration *De tuenda Sacramenti Paenitentiae dignitate,* March 23, 1973: *AAS* 65 (1973) 678; Translation in ICEL, *Documents on the Liturgy, 1963-1979: Conciliar, Papal and Curial Texts* (Collegeville: The Liturgical Press, 1983) (Hereafter cited Liturgical Press), p. 954,

[19]*L'Osservatore Romano,* 24 March 1973, p. 1; Liturgical Press, p. 955.

[20]Ibid.

[21]Pontificia Commissio Codici Iuris Canonici Recognoscendo, *Schema Codicis Iuris Canonici* (Vaticana: Libreria Editrice Vaticana, 1980) (Hereafter cited *1980 Schema),* canon 1340, §1.

[22]Pontificia Commissio Codici Iuris Canonici Recognoscendo, *Relatio* (Typis Polyglottis Vaticanis, 1981).

revised Code was published, not only was there a reference to a *latae sententiae* excommunication, but also once again reference to the excommunication being reserved to the Apostolic See. Since the canons for the revised Code were reviewed by Pope John Paul II, it can only be presumed that the language providing an "automatic excommunication reserved to the Apostolic See" was inserted into the canon so that no one could dispute the seriousness and gravity of the obligation of secrecy regarding the seal of confession.

The language of both codes, likewise, reflects a punitive stance towards confessors who *indirectly* violate confidentiality of oral communications, namely, the seal of confession. The 1917 Code legislated specific penalties for confessors who indirectly violated the seal of confession: suspension from the celebration of Mass and either suspension from hearing sacramental confessions or disqualification for hearing confessions, deprivation of benefices and dignities, deprivation of active and passive vote, and in more serious cases, degradation;[23] while current church law, as has been indicated, states the confessor is to be punished in accord with the seriousness of the offense.[24]

In his commentary on canon 1388 of the revised Code, Green observes that traditionally one of the most severely penalized offenses has been the violation of the seal of confession because of the serious breach of confidentiality of the priest-penitent relationship.[25] Whether the violation of secrecy and betrayal of oral communications to be held confidential be direct or indirect on the part of the confessor, such transgression is to be considered a grave matter. In addition to penalizing the confessor for betrayal of oral communications to be held confidential, the canon also refers to the responsibility of an interpreter and all others privy to confessional knowledge, stating that those who violate such secrecy are to be punished with a just penalty, not

[23]1917 CIC: c. 2368, §1.

[24]c. 1388, §1.

[25]Thomas J. Green, "Title III: Usurpation of Ecclesiastical Functions and Offenses in Their Exercise (cc. 1378-1389)," in *Commentary*, p. 927. See also Kurtscheid, pp. 87, 127, 129, 315 and the commentaries on canon 1388 as found in *Codigo de Derecho Canonico*, Edicion bilingue comentada, 4th ed., edited by Lamberto de Echeverria (Madrid: Biblioteca de Autores Cristianos, 1984), p. 676 and in Lombardia and Arrieta, p. 831.

excluding excommunication. Once again it is clear that there is a serious concern on the part of the Church to preserve and maintain the tradition of confidentiality as it impacts the spoken word within the forum of sacramental confession. It also is clear from historical texts that the seal of confession is one of the oldest examples of historical-theological-canonical protection of oral communications. The fact that the issue of the secrecy of the seal of confession is so well accepted is seen in the fact that so few contemporary sacramental theology texts comment on the importance of the sacramental seal. In reality, the secrecy of the seal is so integral to current theology and canon law, that very little is written on the topic. What is evident in current theological and canonical literature is the *de facto* stance that the seal of confession is inviolable, that confessors, interpreters, and all who in any way are recipients of confessional matter are obliged to secrecy, that persons who reveal confessional material, whether directly or indirectly, are to be punished severely according to church law.

It is clear from these canons, that in addressing secrecy within the internal forum of conscience, canon law is addressing specifically the acquisition of knowledge gained through sacramental confession and, other than mandating secrecy for all involved in sacramental confession, the law is silent regarding confidentiality concerning certain communications exchanged in a non-sacramental setting, such as the extra-sacramental internal forum of spiritual direction, or communications exchanged in marriage counseling, personal counseling, pastoral counseling, or any type of exchange in which there is a spoken or presumed stance that the discussion between the parties involved remain confidential.[26] While the former Code provided for sacramental and extra-sacramental fora within the internal

[26]See James A. Serritella, "Confidentiality, the Church and Clergy," *CLSAP* 48 (1986) 83-93 for a presentation of the various types of civil law problems which can surface when clear guidelines regarding privileged communications are non-existent, as well as suggestions by the author for establishing such guidelines. See also Michael James Callahan, "Historical Inquiry into the Priest-Penitent Privilege," *The Jurist* 36 (1976) 328-337; Ronald P. Stake, "Professionalism and Confidentiality in the Practice of Spiritual Direction," *The Jurist* 43 (1983) 224-232; and William Harold Tiemann and John C. Bush, *The Right to Silence: Privileged Clergy Communication and the Law* (Nashville: Abingdon Press, 1983), pp. 191-192 regarding civil law problems with confidentiality other than priest-penitent privilege.

forum of conscience[27] with the understanding that communications in both the sacramental and extra-sacramental forum demanded "a special and sacred mode of confidentiality,"[28] the revised Code omits this reference to sacramental and extra-sacramental fora within the internal forum. Rather, the language of the revised code clearly speaks to the sacramental forum of conscience, namely confession.

Having addressed the most obvious and well known example of confidential oral communication, that of secrecy surrounding confessional matter, attention will now be turned to the numerous other examples of confidential oral communications within the canonical tradition.

Consultation and Secrecy

In Book I the issue of confidentiality of oral communications is found in the canons governing juridic acts.[29] Canon 127, §3 states:

> All whose consent or counsel is required are obliged to offer their opinion sincerely and, if the seriousness of the matter requires it, to observe secrecy sedulously, and this obligation can be insisted upon by the superior.

Canon 105, §§2, 3 of the 1917 Code contained the same provisions for the possibility of confidentiality of oral communications as does the current law.

Whether counsel or consent is required of a group or of individuals by a superior, be that person a bishop, a pastor, or a religious superior, the opinion is to be offered sincerely, which implicitly acknowledges the right of the group or of the individual "to be fully informed about the matter in question so they can form mature judgments."[30]

Depending on the seriousness of the issue concerning which the superior seeks counsel or consent, that superior can bind to secrecy either the individuals or groups from whom such counsel or consent is sought. This obligation to secrecy can be insisted

[27]1917 CIC: c. 196.

[28]James A. Coriden, "Toward a New Policy for the Church," in *Privacy: A Vanishing Value?*, ed. William C. Bier (New York: Fordham University Press, 1980), p. 389.

[29]cc. 124-128.

[30]Richard A. Hill, "Title VII: Juridic Acts (cc. 124-128)," in *Commentary*, p. 92. See also Thomas J. Green, "Rights and Duties of Diocesan Bishops," *CLSAP* 45 (1983) 21-22 and Sharon Holland, "Internal Governance and Consecrated Life," *CLSAP* 45 (1983) 45.

upon by a superior to the extent of administering an oath of secrecy as was allowed in the 1917 Code,[31] or by issuing a penal precept.[32]

When the law determines that in order to place certain acts a superior requires the consent or counsel of a college or group of persons, the college or group must be convoked, unless particular or proper law provides otherwise when counsel only is sought.[33] Holland[34] and Hill[35] each stress that the exception to convoking a group whose counsel or consent is required is allowed only in cases wherein *counsel* or advice is sought, and only when expressly permitted by proper law. If for example, proper law would allow advice to be sought by means of telephone, such an exception is possible provided the superior does indeed hear the advice of all whose opinions are to be sought. Just as a superior could impose the observation to secrecy upon individuals or groups convoked to give advice, so too could the superior impose secrecy upon any group or individual whose advice was sought by means of telephone interaction.

In light of the fact that the ruling of canon 127, §3 is applicable whenever the superior deems that the seriousness of the matter under consideration requires secrecy, the possibility for obliging secrecy regarding oral communications could impact such diverse groups as: the college of consultors,[36] council of religious institutes,[37] councils of secular institutes,[38] councils of societies of apostolic life,[39] finance councils,[40] the presbyteral council,[41] and such diverse individuals as: interested parties in alienation issues,[42] laity,[43] presbyters,[44] vicars forane or deans,[45] rectors of

[31]1917 CIC: c. 105, §2.

[32]c. 1319. See Hill, p. 92.

[33]c. 127, §1.

[34]Holland, pp. 44-45.

[35]Hill, p. 91.

[36]cc. 494, §§1,2; 1277; 1292, §1.

[37]cc. 638, §3; 647, §§1,2; 656, n.3; 684, §1; 686, §§1,3; 688, §2; 689, §1; 690, §1; 694, §2; 697; 699, §1; 703.

[38]cc. 720; 726; 729; 730.

[39]cc. 743; 744, §1; 745; 746.

[40]cc. 494, §§1,2; 1277; 1292, §1; 1263.

[41]cc. 461, §1; 515, §2; 536, §1; 1215, §2; 1222, §2; 1263.

[42]c. 1292, §1.

[43]c. 524.

[44]Ibid.

[45]Ibid.

neighboring churches.[46] With such a diversity of groups and individuals, issues requiring counsel or consent would also be diverse, as would the type of superior named by the various canons whose responsibility it is to seek the required counsel or consent before placing certain acts. What is common to all groups and individuals is the provision of the law that each superior possesses the authority to oblige individuals or groups to secrecy regarding matters on which opinions have been sought thus preserving confidentiality of oral communication concerning matters the superior believes serious enough to warrant an obligation to secrecy.

Secrecy and Episcopal Candidates

In Book II, "The People of God," there are four canons which specifically address the issue of secrecy regarding oral communications and two which, while not specifically mandating secrecy concerning oral communications, certainly would seem to imply confidentiality of such communication.

The first canon to legislate confidentiality of oral communication in Book II concerns the surfacing of names of presbyters considered to be suitable candidates for the episcopacy. Canon 377, §2 states:

> At least every three years the bishops of an ecclesiastical province, or if circumstances suggest this, the bishops of a conference of bishops are to compose in common counsel and in secret a list of presbyters, including members of institutes of consecrated life, who are suitable for the episcopacy and send it to the Apostolic See; each bishop retains the right to make known to the Apostolic See on his own the names of presbyters whom he thinks worthy and suitable for the episcopal office.

This canon was not in the 1917 Code. Rather, the 1917 Code indicated that before a person was raised to the episcopacy, his suitability had to be approved in a manner determined by the Apostolic See,[47] then proceeded to list the required qualities

[46] c. 1215, §2.
[47] 1917 CIC: c. 330.

of a candidate for the episcopate,[48] but did not define in universal law the role of bishops in raising names of possible candidates. The role of bishops within an ecclesiastical province or in a conference of bishops is set forth in the documents issued after the Second Vatican Council, namely *Ecclesiae Sanctae*[49] and the "Norms for Selection of Candidates for the Episcopacy in the Latin Church."[50] While both documents stress the importance of secrecy, the norms expressly indicate why secrecy is so important in the surfacing of names of candidates and in any discussion of such candidates.

> In the expediting of all these matters, the prescribed so-called papal secret must be strictly observed by the bishops, the papal legate, the priests and the laity who in any way whatever have part. This is demanded by the very nature of the matter and by the respect due to the persons under consideration.[51]

It is interesting to note that in the United States, a decree predating both the Second Vatican Council and the 1917 Code contained similar provisions as the current law as regards both the role of bishops in surfacing names of possible candidates and in the importance of secrecy in discussing the names of any possible candidates.[52] These same norms with provisions for secrecy in surfacing names of candidates for episcopacy were reiterated in post 1917 codal decrees issued to the bishops of Canada and Newfoundland,[53] Scotland,[54] Brazil,[55] Mexico,[56] and Poland.[57]

[48]1917 CIC: c. 331, §1.

[49]Paul VI, apostolic letter, August 6, 1966: *AAS* 58 (1966) 757-758. Translation in Austin Flannery, ed., *Vatican II: The Conciliar and Post Conciliar Documents* (Northport, New York: Costello Publishing Company, 1975), 1: 597.

[50]Consilii pro Publicis Ecclesiae Negotiis, *Episcoporum delectum*, March 25, 1972: *AAS* 64 (1972) 386-391. Translation in *CLD* 7: 366-373.

[51]*Episcoporum delectum*, art. 14, *AAS* 64 at 391; *CLD* 7: 372.

[52]Sacrae Congregatio Consistorialis, decree *Circa proponendos ad episcopale ministerium in Foederatis Americae Septentrionalis Statibus*, July 25, 1916: *AAS* 8 (1916) 400-404, at 401-402. Translation in *CLD* I: 194-198, at 195-195.

[53]Ibid., decree *Circa proponendos ad episcopale ministerium in Canadensi Dominio et Terrae Novae Insulis*, March 19, 1919: *AAS* 11 (1919) 124-128, at 125-126.

[54]Ibid., decree *Circa proponendos ad episcopale ministerium in Scotia*, November 20, 1920: *AAS* 13 (1921) 13-16, at 14.

[55]Ibid., decree *Circa proponendos ad episcopale ministerium in Brasilia*, March 19, 1921: *AAS* 13 (1921) 222-225, at 223-224.

[56]Ibid., decree *Circa proponendos ad episcopale ministerium in Mexicana Republica*, April 4, 1921: *AAS* 13 (1921) 379-383, at 380.

[57]Ibid, decree *Circa proponendos ad episcopale ministerium pro dioecesibus ritus Latini in Polanis*, August 20, 1921: *AAS* 13 (1921) 430-432, at 430-431.

These documents reveal that in the process of surfacing names of candidates suitable for the episcopacy, a tradition of confidentiality of oral communications is both consistent and evident. The secrecy surrounding the entire discussion of names surfaced by bishops was mandated in the guidelines of the Sacred Consistorial Congregation, whether the discussion took place between bishop or archbishop and diocesan consultors, between bishop or archbishop and irremovable pastors, between bishop or archbishop and regular clergy, or between the bishops themselves. To insure confidentiality concerning inquiries made by bishop or archbishop to consultors and pastors, the bishop or archbishop was to consult each as an individual and to impose an obligation of secrecy upon each person consulted. The bishops were to disclose to no one except other bishops, and only at their regularly scheduled meeting, any information received through consultation. To insure confidentiality concerning names surfaced, the bishops were to take an oath of secrecy while at their meeting. Therefore, the obligation to secrecy as legislated in the revised Code both reiterates and continues the tradition of confidentiality relative to discussion of names under consideration for the episcopacy.

The second canon of Book II requiring confidentiality of oral communications is also concerned with secrecy in the surfacing names of candidates suitable for the episcopacy, and in this instance affects the pontifical legate.

> Unless other provisions have legitimately been made, whenever a diocesan bishop or a coadjutor bishop is to be named, in regard to the *ternus,* as it is called, to be proposed to the Apostolic See it is the responsibility of the pontifical legate to seek out individually the suggestions of the metropolitan and the suffragans of the province to which the diocese to be provided belongs or with which it is joined and of the president of the conference of bishops and to communicate them to the Apostolic See together (with) his own preference; moreover, the pontifical legate is to hear some members of the college of consultors and of the cathedral chapter, and if he judges it expedient, he shall also obtain, individually and in secret, the opinion of other members of the secular and religious clergy as well as of the laity who are outstanding for their

wisdom.[58]

As with canon 377, §2, this canon did not exist in the 1917 Code. Likewise, when the 1980 *Schema* was published, canon 344, §3 of that *Schema* focused only on the bishops of the province. Nothing was said of the role of the pontifical legate. Provision for the role of the legate is incorporated into the 1982 *Schema,*[59] even though there is no discussion of such recorded in the 1981 *Relatio.* The wording of canon 377, §3 of the 1982 *Schema* is the same as that of the revised Code. However, provisions governing involvement of the pontifical legate in seeking opinions of ecclesiastics and qualified laity regarding names of possible candidates for the episcopacy were issued by Pope Paul VI in his *motu proprio* on papal legates[60] and by the Council for Public Affairs of the Church in their norms for the promotion of candidates to the episcopal ministry in the church.[61] Both documents, which predate the *schemata* and the *Relatio,* enjoined the pontifical legate to seek out the opinion of ecclesiastics as well as members of the laity who seemed best qualified to provide useful and trustworthy information; and seeking such information demanded that secrecy be observed.[62] Canon 377, §3 basically reiterates the provisions of these two documents regarding the importance of secrecy in seeking such opinions. Thomas J. Green believes that the seeking of opinions from the individuals mentioned in the canon seems necessary if the pontifical legate is

> ...to benefit from the diversified insights of a reasonably broad cross-section of the people of God in a particular church. In a matter of such noteworthy importance for the life and mission of that church the informed involvement of at least select clergy, religious, and laity seems indispensable.[63]

[58]c, 377, §3.

[59]Pontificia Commissio Codici Iuris Canonici Recognoscendo, *Codicis Iuris Canonici Schema Novissimum Iuxta Placita Patrum Commissionis Emendatum atque Summo Pontifici Praesentatum* (Typis Polyglottis Vaticanis, 1982), canon 377, §3.

[60]Paul VI, motu proprio *Sollicitudo omnium ecclesiarum, June 24, 1969: AAS* 61 (1969) 473-484. Translation in *CLD* 7: 277-284.

[61]See footnote 50, *supra.*

[62]*Solicitudo,* art. 6, §2a, *AAS* 61 at 481; *CLD* 7: 280; *Episcoporum delectum,* arts 12, 13, §§1,2, 14, *AAS* 64 at 390-391; *CLD* 7: 371-372.

[63]Thomas J. Green, "Chapter II: Bishops (cc. 375-411)," in *Commentary,* p. 322.

As to the importance of secrecy in obtaining the opinions of the above-mentioned persons, Green observed that presumably the requirement of secrecy is twofold: 1) to preclude any semblance of political campaigning that might violate the integrity of the process; and, 2) to protect the value of confidentiality and respect for persons in such a delicate area.[64]

While canon 377, §3, like canon 377, §2 might be new to the revised Code, it is the fruit of ecclesial documentation which predates the 1983 Code. The confidentiality of oral communications as required by canon 377, §3 reflects the same respect for secrecy that is found in prior ecclesial documentation affecting surfacing of names and suitability of candidates to the episcopacy.

Secrecy in the Diocesan Curia

In addition to imposing secrecy upon all involved in the process of surfacing of names of candidates considered suitable for the episcopacy, and in the discussion of qualities of such candidates, the law also provides that all persons appointed by the diocesan bishop to exercise offices within the diocesan curia must observe secrecy within the limits and according to the manner determined by law or by the bishop.[65] This canon basically repeats canon 364, §2 of the former Code, but unlike the former Code, current law no longer mandates taking an oath in the hands of the bishop. Rather, the obligation of secrecy is attached to the acceptance of the office. Likewise, the former Code specifically listed the personnel of the diocesan curia: vicar general, officialis, chancellor, promoter of justice, defender of the bond, synodal judges and examiners, pastor consultors, auditors, notaries, couriers, and constables,[66] who, in turn, were bound by this oath of secrecy. The revised Code, however, simply states that the diocesan curia consists of those institutions and persons which furnish assistance to the bishop,[67] thus leaving to the diocesan bishop identification of membership in the curia. During the course of the revision process, the *coetus* indicated that

[64]Ibid.
[65]c. 471, n.2.
[66]1917 CIC: c. 365.
[67]c. 469.

the diocesan curia consisted of the vicar general or episcopal vicar, chancellors, notaries and episcopal archivist, diocesan examiners, finance officer and finance council.[68] While the revised Code contains no such listing, John Alesandro believes membership in the curia does include some of those persons mentioned under the former Code as well as persons and groups mentioned during the revision process, and various institutions and persons furnishing assistance to the bishop in the governance of a diocese.

> ... The curia certainly includes the vicars general and episcopal vicars, the chancellor and other notaries, the tribunal personnel, and the finance officer. It would also seem to include the finance council, specifically treated in article 3. The three articles of this chapter, however, do not offer a taxative list. Given the Code's concept of ecclesiastical office (c. 145), all those who participate in the overall administration of the diocese should be considered members of the diocesan curia, especially those who direct diocesan departments such as education, religious education, liturgy, charity, social concerns, temporalities, and the other facets of ecclesial life organized and promoted at the diocesan level. The presbyteral council and the college of consultors, which are treated in a separate chapter are not, strictly speaking, institutes of the curia, although they are closely associated with it insofar as their counsel assists the bishop in the governance of the diocese (c. 495). ... Pastors constituted by the presbyteral council to advise the bishop regarding the administrative removal or transfer of a pastor (cc. 1740-1752), are similar to the examiners and parish priest consultors of the former Code. They too are considered members of the diocesan curia even though their involvement in diocesan administration will be rather infrequent.[69]

With such an expanded notion of membership in the diocesan curia obviously far more persons would be expected to observe

[68]*Communicationes* 9 (1977) 254.

[69]John A. Alesandro, "Chapter II: The Diocesan Curia (cc. 469-494)," in *Commentary*, p. 383.

secrecy as it is demanded by law or by the bishop than was envisioned in the former Code's delineation. The revised Code clearly reiterates the importance of secrecy in the exercise of responsibilities pertinent to the uniqueness of each office when it provides that the observance of secrecy is attached to the acceptance of an office. In reviewing the possibility for membership in the diocesan curia, the scope of the work, would, by its very nature, include discussion, opinion-seeking, critiquing, reporting, challenging, and refining matters under consideration. When the law or the bishop indicate that secrecy is to be observed regarding any verbal exchange among members of the diocesan curia who function as individuals or as a group, the tradition of honoring confidentiality of oral communications is being practiced.

Secrecy in Religious Institutes

The next canon from Book II which protects the secrecy of oral communications is canon 645, §4 governing the role of superiors in the admission of candidates to a religious institute. The first three paragraphs of that canon indicate the type of testimony required by an institute before a candidate is to be admitted, namely, proofs of baptism, confirmation, and the free status of a prospective candidate and testimonials indicative of a candidate's character, freedom from impediments, stability, and suitability for the religious institute.[70] Paragraph four of the canon states: "If it appears necessary superiors can ask for other information, even with the obligation of secrecy." Since superiors are responsible for admitting candidates, they, therefore have a serious obligation to be knowledgeable about persons seeking admittance. In order to be reasonably certain of a candidate's health, character, suitability, stability, capability, adaptability, and freedom from impediments, the law empowers superiors to obtain in a secret manner any additional information that would help a religious superior resolve any serious doubts about a candidate. Since the law specifically utilizes the word "information" rather than "documentation," such additional information could be any informational exchange, including verbal, which a superior

[70] c. 645, §§1-3.

believes is wise and prudent to procure in order to make a good decision, that is not otherwise required by canon law, proper law, or even other institute regulations, statutes, or policies.[71] In his commentary on canon 645, §4, Jordon Hite points to an important distinction in the law, namely, that in asking for additional information, it is the methodology that is secret, that is, the candidate is unaware that the superior is seeking certain information, which is quite different from attempting to obtain secret information, which the canon does not permit.[72] What is crucial to the issue of confidentiality is the freedom of a religious superior to obtain secretly whatever information is necessary to remove doubts as to a candidate's suitability. In turn, the confidential nature of this information secretly obtained, demands great reverance, discretion, and sensitivity on the part of the recipients.[73] The former Code not only demanded testimonials indicative of the freedom and suitability of a prospective candidate[74] and empowered the superior to conduct secret inquiries concerning such qualities in a candidate,[75] but also obliged superiors to keep secret both the information received and the names of persons who furnished it. Canon 645, §4 of the revised Code, then, synthesizes the laws of the former Code regarding the freedom of a superior to ask for any necessary information regarding a candidate seeking admission to a religious institute, and while the revised Code does not legislate secrecy regarding information received, but only the manner in which a superior may obtain additional information, the canonical tradition of

[71]Jordan Hite, "Admission of Candidates and Formation of Members: Canons 641-661," in *A Handbook of Canons 573-746,* eds., Jordon Hite, Sharon Holland, and Daniel Ward (Collegeville: The Liturgical Press, 1985) (Hereafter cited *Handbook*), p. 131.

[72]Ibid. The author gives as an example of secretly seeking information a case wherein a candidate might be suspected of hiding a criminal record. The candidate has stated that he or she has never been convicted, but someone who knows the candidate has stated otherwise. The superior could secretly seek information regarding such a conviction instead of embarrassing the candidate or the institute in case the person who made the statement about the conviction is mistaken.

[73]Rose McDermott, "Chapter III: Admission of Candidates and Formation of Membership (cc. 641-661)," in *Commentary,* p. 491. See also Sharon Holland, "Select Questions in Religious Law: Admission, Separation, Approbation," *CLSAP* 44 (1982) 122, and Pio Vito Pinto, ed., *Commento al Codice di Diritto Canonico* (Rome: Urbaniana University Press, 1985), p. 393.

[74]1917 CIC: c. 544, §6.

[75]1917 CIC: c. 545, §4.

secrecy as articulated in the former Code as well as the confidential nature of the information received demands secrecy.

As indicated in the opening paragraph addressing the issue of confidentiality of oral communications in the canons on the "People of God," two canons, while not demanding secrecy directly, certainly imply secrecy indirectly.

Canon 630, §5 exhorts members of religious communities to approach superiors with trust, to whom they can express their minds freely and willingly. However, the law forbids such superiors to induce their subjects in any way whatever to make a manifestation of conscience.[76] If a member of a religious community is to approach a superior with trust, the connotation of such an exhortation is that the superior is trustworthy and will hold the conversation in confidence. If per chance a manifestation of conscience is voluntarily made, the superior may not reveal this matter in the external forum without the consent of the subject.[77] Richard McBrien strongly asserts:

> . . . if a superior, through the "manifestation of conscience," properly or improperly should come into possession of knowledge damaging to the person involved-even if for example, such knowledge could disqualify the person from vows or sacred orders–the superior's hands are tied. Only the subject could loose them.[78]

Francis Morrisey believes there should be clear parameters established when a superior is conversing with a candidate so that the candidate knows whether or not the information imparted will be used eventually in reaching a decision regarding the candidate's suitability for the specific vocation in question.[79]

[76]Jordan F. Hite ("Chapter II: The Governance of Institutes (cc. 617-640)," in *Commentary*, p. 483.) states that manifestation of conscience includes all matters of the interior life from the highest grace to sinful matters. It does not include the external conduct of the member, most especially that required for fidelity to the life of the community contained in the proper law of the institute.

[77]Ibid. See also John C. Ford, "Religious Superiors, Subjects and Psychiatrists," *Catholic Theological Society of America Proceedings* 17 (1962) 86.

[78]Richard P. McBrien, "The Believer's Right to Privacy," in *Privacy: A Vanishing Value?*, ed. William C. Bier (New York: Fordham University Press, 1980), p. 126.

[79]Francis G. Morrisey, "Issue of Confidentiality in Religious Life," *Bulletin on Issues in Religious Law* 4 (1988) 8. See also Richard A. Hill, "Spiritual Directors and Governance-1," *Review for Religious* 47 (1988) 624, 626-628 regarding the issue of parameters when a superior, member of a council or formation director is also a candidate's spiritual director.

If a candidate knows ahead of time that any or all information conveyed to a superior could be brought into discussion regarding said candidate's suitability, the dimension of freedom and trust could easily be diminished.

The general thrust of this canon was found in canon 530, § §1, 2 of the former Code with similar injunctions as to reservedness and carefulness on the part of the superior regarding material transmitted,[80] as well as injunctions against inducing subjects in any manner whatsoever to make a manifestation of conscience to a superior.[81]

Therefore, while canon 630, §5 of the revised Code does not legislate specifically the importance of confidentiality of these oral communications, it is obvious that confidentiality is important, and if such cannot be honored, then the candidate or member should be informed of that reality in order to make an informed decision as to whether or not matters of a confidential nature will be entrusted to a superior.

A further example of a canon affecting the People of God, which, while not specifically mandating secrecy, implies such is canon 642.

> Superiors are to be vigilant about admitting only those who, besides the required age, have health, suitable character and sufficient qualities of maturity to embrace the particular life of the institute; this health, character, and maturity are to be attested to, if necessary by using experts, with due regard for the prescription of canon 220.

Canon 220 to which this canon refers states that no one is permitted to damage unlawfully the good reputation which another person enjoys nor to violate the right of other persons to protect their own privacy.

In the admission of candidates to an institute three aspects of a person are to be verified: the health of a candidate, the character of the person, and the candidate's maturity to embrace the particular life of an institute. These qualities can be verified, if necessary by using experts, with due regard for canon

[80]Joseph Creusen and Adam C. Ellis, *Religious Men and Women in Church Law* (Milwaukee: The Bruce Publishing Company, 1958), p. 103.

[81]Ibid., at 101. See also Woywod-Smith, 1: 201.

220. Such information could be verified by means of interviews with the candidate and psychological testing and physical examination of the candidate. The canon specifies that the institute or experts employed by the institute are to conduct their examination without prejudice to the individual's right to protection of privacy. Jordon Hite observes that this is an important consideration for institutes to use in guiding experts so that they do not use methods that would violate privacy or in any way harm the reputation of the institute.[82] In whatever manner examinations, interviews, and testing are conducted in order that such qualities are verified, Hite exhorts institutes to

> . . . obtain the proper releases to review the data from both medical examinations and psychological testing, which should ensure a candidate that the information will be kept confidential. The release or an accompanying explanation should clearly state the purpose of the examination, who is to see the report, and what happens to the report after its initial use. In some cases the report may be given to the superior and/or council, while at the same time the candidate is given a copy of the report or a "read out" of its contents. It is helpful for the psychologist to instruct those who will read the report on the nature, uses, and limitations of the information in the report.
>
> . . . In some cases these reports are shared with formation directors so they can better understand the candidate and more skillfully promote growth and development. If this is the case, it should be explained to the candidate and permission secured.[83]

Any discussion of issues surfaced as a result of the physical examination or the psychological test and interview, or discussion of issues surfaced by a candidate with a superior, which, in turn, reveal some aspect of that person's character, or emotional, psychological, spiritual, or affective maturity likewise ought to be respectful of a person's privacy and reputation. Each institute, therefore, needs to make provisions as to who in positions of institute governance would be privy to the information exchanged during such discussions between superior and candidate and to extend the parameters regarding individual recipient of oral

[82]Hite, *Handbook,* p. 119.
[83]Ibid.

communications considered to be confidential only when a proportionate reason requires such an extension.[84] If proper law states that in the admission of candidates, superiors are required to obtain the advice or consent of the council, the superior could insist upon secrecy even to the extent of administering an oath, as the superior is empowered to do, since the issues under consideration are serious.[85] However, when the issue no longer is one of extending the parameters regarding recipients of oral communication, but rather one of violation of a candidate's privacy, Hite expressly states:

> ...If there is information which an institute cannot have except by violating or seeming to violate an individual's right to privacy, it should forego seeking the information, but it should not place itself at a disadvantage by granting admission on inconclusive evidence of suitability.[86]

Thus, while canon 642 does not mandate specifically confidentiality regarding these oral communications concerning a candidate's health, character, and maturity, the scope and sensitivity of information entailed in such an investigation, as well as the law's twofold concern for not damaging unlawfully the good reputation a person enjoys, nor violating the right of persons to protect their privacy, connotes an attitude of respect for confidentiality of oral communications between prospective candidates and superiors of religious institutes.

Secret Marriages

In Book IV, "The Sanctifying Office of the Church," are found the canons governing secrecy in the celebration of the sacraments of penance and marriage. The canons on penance having been addressed, the issue of secrecy as it impacts upon the celebration of marriage will now be examined. Usually marriages are public celebrations; however, the law does provide for the possibility of secret marriages. Canon 1130 provides: "For a serious and urgent reason the local ordinary can permit a marriage to be celebrated secretly." While canonical form is to be followed in the celebration of a secret marriage, banns, if they are in force in an area, are not to be announced and the ceremony itself

[84]Morrisey, p. 5.
[85]c. 127, §3.
[86]Hite, *Handbook*, p. 120.

takes place in secret, and all involved are to keep the fact of the marriage a secret. In deciding whether permission should be granted for the purpose of celebrating a marriage secretly, the law mandates that there be a "serious and urgent reason." Thomas P. Doyle exhorts that the seriousness of the situation should be such that the good achieved by a public celebration is sufficiently offset by the good to be achieved by a secret celebration.[87] Commentators state that serious issues would include: living in concubinage; marriages which are contrary to civil law, yet the prohibition of such is contrary to natural or ecclesiastical law, such as interracial marriages; disparity of social status among spouses; irrational or unreasonable opposition of parents; marriages between widowed persons or military officers who would lose either benefits or position if the marriage is known publicly; and marriages in countries where the Church is persecuted and religious marriages are forbidden.[88] Likewise, there must be urgency to the situation which means that possible harm could come to the parties if there is a delay in marrying.[89]

Once there is permission to celebrate a marriage secretly, such permission includes permission to conduct the pre-marital investigation secretly, and also obliges that secrecy concerning the marriage be observed by the local ordinary, the assisting minister, the witnesses, and the spouses.[90] This grave obligation of secrecy was equally binding in the 1917 Code.[91] The obligation to secrecy demanded by the law is in favor of the parties. Should they both choose to make the fact of their marriage known at sometime after the celebration, the obligation of

[87]Thomas P. Doyle, "Chapter VII: Marriages Secretly Celebrated (cc. 1130-1133)," in *Commentary*, p. 807.

[88]Ibid. See also de Echeverria, p. 550 and Lombardia and Arrieta, p. 688. Several commentators on the 1917 Code treated the same issues as examples of serious reasons for permitting a marriage to be celebrated secretly: John A. Abbo and Jerome D. Hannan (*The Sacred Canons* (St. Louis: B. Herder Book Co., 1952)), 2: 364; P. Charles Augustine (*A Commentary on Canon Law* (St. Louis: B. Herder Book Co., 1935)), 5: 316-317; T. Lincoln Bouscaren and Adam C. Ellis, (*Canon Law: A Text and Commentary*, second edition revised (Milwaukee: The Bruce Publishing Company, 1951)), p. 590; Felix M. Cappello (*Tractatus Canonico-Moralis De Sacramentis*, vol. V, "De Matrimonio" (Romae: Marietti Editori Ltd., 1950)), p. 708; Woywod-Smith, 1: 696.

[89]Doyle, p. 807.

[90]c. 1131, §§1,2.

[91]1917 CIC: c. 1105.

secrecy ceases.[92] Since the obligation to secrecy is in favor of the parties, anyone not mentioned in the Code who also becomes aware of the marriage is bound to secrecy.[93] Likewise, since the obligation to secrecy is in favor of the parties, the local ordinary has a right to exercise discretion in the choice of witnesses, taking care that those chosen are persons who will understand the nature of the secret celebration and will, in turn, observe secrecy.[94]

While there is articulated within the law a grave obligation to observe ongoing secrecy regarding marriages which are celebrated secretly, there are circumstances in the law under which such an obligation ceases. If serious scandal or serious harm to the sanctity of the marriage is threatened by observing secrecy then the obligation to observe secrecy on the part of the local ordinary ceases. Such a possibility for cessation of the obligation of secrecy is to be made known to the parties before the celebration of the marriage.[95] Unlike canon 1131, §2 which obliges both spouses to secrecy, with the canonical understanding that one party cannot, without the consent of the other, break secrecy and reveal the fact of their marriage, canon 1132 permits the local ordinary to make the decision regarding cessation of the obligation of secrecy without the consent of the parties.

> He may do so if he judges that continued secrecy will cause serious scandal which could be averted by publishing the marriage, e.g. when the parties are known to be living together and at the same time actively participating in the life of the Church. He may also publicize the marriage if he judges that serious harm will be done to the sanctity of marriage by continuing secrecy about the marriage.[96]

Canon 1106 of the former Code specifically stated that one of the reasons for cessation of secrecy was if when children were

[92]Doyle, p. 807. See also Woywod-Smith, 1: 696-697.

[93]Doyle, p. 807.

[94]Ibid.

[95]c. 1132. The 1917 Code also provided for cessation of secrecy if the keeping of the secret would cause great scandal or gravely impair the sanctity of the marriage, but it did not make provisions for informing the parties of the reasons for cessation of secrecy.

[96]Doyle, p. 807.

born, the parents did not have them baptized, or if the parents neglected the Christian education of their children. During the revision process the *coetus* studying matrimony specifically rejected a request to reinstate in the revised Code this provision as the members felt such a norm was no longer opportune within the present socio-religious context.[97] The *coetus,* however, did choose to add to the formulation of the revised canon the final phrase concerning making known to the parties the possibility of and reasons for cessation of secrecy.[98] Such an addition would seem to enhance the respect for secrecy accorded the parties since marriage in secret is allowable only for serious and urgent reasons, so also would the observance of such secrecy cease only because of serious reasons. Therefore, it is out of respect for the parties they be told of such a possibility. Ladislas Orsy believes the local ordinary should consult with the couple before any revelation is made.[99] In reviewing the canons on marriages which take place in secret, it is clear that in this area there is a tradition of confidentiality of oral communications, both in whatever is spoken during preparation of the parties for marriage and in the actual ceremony, and that confidentiality concerning the marriage extends to the local ordinary, the assisting minister, witnesses, spouses, and all who hear of the marriage. Confidentiality surrounding this matter ceases either when the local ordinary believes that serious scandal or serious harm will impringe upon the sanctity of marriage if the secret perdures, or the spouses themselves jointly decide to reveal the marriage.

Secrecy in Tribunals

Within Book VII, "Processes," there are several references to confidentiality impacting oral communications.

In the canons governing the discipline to be observed in tribunals in penal and contentious cases, judges and tribunal personnel are bound to secrecy and the judge can bind by oath to preserve such secrecy both court personnel and the parties involved in either penal or contentious cases.

[97] *Communicationes* 10 (1978) 102-103.

[98] Ibid., at 102.

[99] Ladislas Orsy, *Marriage in Canon Law* (Wilmington, Delaware: Michael Glazier, Inc., 1986), p. 199.

> Judges and tribunal personnel are always bound to secrecy of office in a penal case; they are also thus bound in a contentious case if the parties may be harmed by the revelation of some procedural act.
>
> They are also always bound to observe secrecy concerning the discussion among the judges in a collegiate tribunal before passing the sentence and concerning the various notes and opinions offered during the discussion...
>
> Moreover, as often as the nature of a case or the proofs is such that the reputation of others is endangered by divulging the acts or proofs, or an opportunity for discord is provided or scandal or some other similar disadvantage might arise, the judge can bind the witnesses, the experts, the parties and their advocates or proxies by oath to observe secrecy.[100]

This canon basically repeats canon 1623, §§1-3 of the former Code. The sense of the canon is that the officers of the court may not discuss the case with any third party, meaning, any party not having legitimate access to the acts.[101] Since the law provides for legitimate access to the acts, namely, canons 1470, §1 and 1598, §1, canon 1455, §§1-3 specifically deals with persons *not* having legitimate access. This canon also highlights the importance of what Lombardia and Arrieta term "official" or "professional" secrecy among tribunal staff members in that all tribunal personnel are expected to maintain confidentiality and guard secrecy by refraining from any discussion of facts of the case with a third party or divulging information which could damage a person's reputation or lead to discord or scandal.[102]

Since paragraph two of the canon mandates secrecy concerning discussion among judges in a collegiate tribunal relevant to opinions offered during said discussion, the specifics outlined in canon 1609, §3 regarding discussion of determinants to be included in the dispositive part of a sentence are likewise governed by the obligation of secrecy. Similarly, since the disciplinary

[100]c. 1455, §§1,2,3.

[101]Lawrence G. Wrenn, "Title III: The Discipline to be Observed in Tribunals (cc. 1446-1457)," in *Commentary,* p. 962.

[102]Lombardia and Arrieta, p. 877.

canons apply to contentious procedures, the directives of canon 1455, §1 and 1455, §3 would apply to any discussions and verbal proceedings which would take place during the oral contentious process[103] should the nature of the case or proofs surfaced endanger the reputation of the parties or give rise to an opportunity for discord or scandal.

A further canon of Book VII which addresses the issue of confidentiality of oral communications is also among those canons governing disciplinary procedures to be observed in tribunals and penalizes judges who violate the law of secrecy, stating they can be punished by the competent authority with fitting penalties, including deprivation of office.[104] In addition to the judge being punished for violation of secrecy, the law empowers the judge to punish officers and personnel of the tribunal if one of them should violate the law of secrecy.[105] Provisions for punishing judge, officers, and other personnel for violating the law of secrecy were likewise present in the former Code.[106] During the course of the revision process a consultor suggested that canon 1457, §1 be transferred to the canons on penalties, but after a brief discussion, the *coetus* decided the above-mentioned canon should remain in its place within the disciplinary canons.[107]

The fact that the former Code in its canons on discipline within the tribunal provided for punishment of judge and tribunal personnel who violated secrecy, the fact that during the revision process a *coetus* discussion as to whether or not this clear articulation of punishment for violation of secrecy should be moved to the canons on penalties resulted in retaining the canon within the same context as the former code, the fact that neither the placement of the canon nor the stringent regulations regarding secrecy were altered during the final review of the proposed code, all seem to confirm the importance of confidentiality of oral communications regarding both discussion of cases among judges, and in revelation of harmful information either by judges or tribunal personnel.

[103]cc. 1656-1670.
[104]c. 1457, §1.
[105]c. 1457, §2.
[106]1917 CIC: c. 1625.
[107]*Communicationes* 10 (1978) 255.

In the gathering of proofs within processes, the law exempts from being called as witnesses persons who have been recipients of confidential communication, namely, clerics in regard to whatever was made known to them in connection with their sacred ministry, that is, "professional secrets learned apart from the confessional;"[108] and, civil officials, doctors, obstetricians, advocates, notaries and others bound by professional secrecy, even by reason of advice rendered, as regards matters subject to this secrecy.[109] This canon basically repeats provisions for confidentiality of oral communications as found in canon 1755, §2, n. 1 of the former Code. During the revision process a suggestion was made to admit as witnesses persons heretofore exempted from testifying, but the consultors envisioned the danger in allowing such a practice;[110] therefore provisions were retained for exempting as witnesses persons who were recipients of confidential information. The fact that there appeared to be no further discussion within the *coetus* regarding modifying the respect for secrecy of confidential communications, nor did there appear to be any discussion among the consultors to the October, 1981, Plenaria meeting regarding alteration of the previously exempted status of persons who were recipients of confidential communications, as well as the fact that the canon has remained basically the same from its articulation in the former Code, through the revision process, to its format in the revised Code in its preservation of exemption as witnesses recipients of confidential communications, speaks to the tradition of confidentiality of oral communications. Should the court decide to seek the testimony of persons bound by professional secrecy, such as counselors, physicians, psychiatrists, psychologists, social workers, canonical injunctions regarding authorized release of information held by such persons are to be observed prior to obtaining their testimony.[111] No matter how valuable or necessary the information possessed by an exempted witness, the law protects

[108]Francis Wanenmacher, *Canonical Evidence in Marriage Cases* (Philadelphia: Dolphin Press, 1935), p. 131.

[109]c. 1548, §2, n.1.

[110]*Communicationes* 11 (1979) 109.

[111]Sacra Congregatio de Disciplina Sacramentorum, Instruction *Provida Mater Ecclesia,* August 15, 1936: *AAS* 28 (1936) 313-372, art. 121, §2, n. 1. at 338. Translation in *CLD* 2: 471-529, at 501-502.

the client-professional confidentiality, and therefore the court could not demand that one of these witnesses testify without an authorized release from the party or parties with whom the professional interacted. Likewise, should one of the exempted witnesses believe he or she could not testify even though in possession of a professional release, the court could not force a given witness to testify.[112] Such a provision serves to enhance further the importance of confidentiality of oral communications within the canonical tradition.

Conclusion

While the issue of confidentiality of oral communications within canon law could be complicated by civil legislation which varies from place to place and must be taken into consideration, it is clear that there exists within the universal law of the Church, a tradition respectful of confidentiality concerning oral communications.

[112]William M. Van Ommeren, *Mental Illness Affecting Matrimonial Consent,* Canon Law Studies, 415 (Washington: The Catholic University of America, 1961), p. 197.

SELECT BIBLIOGRAPHY

Sources

Bier, William C. *Privacy: A Vanishing Value?* New York: Fordham University Press, Inc., 1980.

Coriden, James A. et al., eds. *The Code of Canon Law: A Text and Commentary.* New York/Mahwah: Paulist Press, 1985.

de Echeverria, Lamberto, ed. *Codigo de Derecho Canonico.* Edicion bilingue comentada. Cuarta edicion. Madrid: Biblioteca de Autores Cristianos, 1984.

Hite, Jordan F.; Holland, Sharon; and Ward, Daniel, eds. *A Handbook of Canons 573-746.* Collegeville: The Liturgical Press, 1985.

Kurtscheid, Bertrand. *A History of the Seal of Confession.* Translated by F.A. Marks. St. Louis, MO: B. Herder Book Co., 1927.

Lombardia, Pedro, y. Arrieta, Juan Ignacio, eds. *Codigo de Derecho Canonico.* Edicion Anotada. Pamplona: Ediciones Universidad de Navarra, S.A., 1983.

Orsy, Ladislas. *Marriage in Canon Law.* Wilmington, Delaware: Michael Glazier, Inc., 1986.

Roos, John R. *The Seal of Confession.* Canon Law Studies, 413. Washington: The Catholic University of America, 1960.

Van Ommeren, William M. *Mental Illness Affecting Matrimonial Consent.* Canon Law Studies, 415. Washington: The Catholic University of America, 1961.

Wanenmacher, Francis. *Canonical Evidence in Marriage Cases.* Philadelphia: Dolphin Press, 1935.

Woywod, Stanislaus. Revised by Callistus Smith. *A Practical Commentary on the Code of Canon Law.* 2 vols. New York: Joseph F. Wagner, Inc., 1943.

Articles

Alesandro, John A. "Chapter II: The Diocesan Curia (cc. 469-494)." In *The Code of Canon Law: A Text and Commentary,* edited by James A. Coriden et al., 382-400. New York/Mahwah: Paulist Press, 1985.

Coriden, James A. "Toward a New Policy for the Church." In *Privacy: A Vanishing Value?,* edited by William C. Bier, 387-398. New York: Fordham University Press, 1980.

Doyle, Thomas P. "Chapter VII: Marriages Secretly Celebrated (cc. 1130-1133)." In *The Code of Canon Law: A Text and Commentary,* edited by James A. Coriden et al., 806-807. New York/Mahwah: Paulist Press, 1985.

Ford, John C. "Religious Superiors, Subjects and Psychiatrists." *Catholic Theological Society of America Proceedings* 17 (1962) 63-129.

Green, Thomas J. "Chapter II: Bishops (cc. 375-411)." In *The Code of Canon Law: A Text and Commentary,* edited by James A. Coriden et al., 319-341. New York/Mahwah: Paulist Press, 1985.

______________. "Rights and Duties of Diocesan Bishops." *CLSA Proceedings* 45 (1983) 18-36.

______________. "Title III: Usurpation of Ecclesiastical Functions and Offenses in Their Exercise (cc. 1378-1379)." In *The Code of Canon Law: A Text and Commentary,* edited by James A. Coriden et al., 924-928. New York/Mahwah: Paulist Press, 1985.

Hill, Richard A., "Title VII: Juridic Acts (cc. 124-128)." In *The Code of Canon Law: A Text and Commentary,* edited by James A. Coriden et al., 89-92. New York/Mahwah: Paulist Press, 1985.

______________. "Spiritual Directors and Governance-1." *Review for Religious* 47 (1988) 623-628.

Hite, Jordan. "Admission of Candidates and Formation of Members: Canons 641-661." In *A Handbook on Canons 573-746,* edited by Jordan Hite, Sharon Holland, and Daniel Ward, 115-168. Collegeville: The Liturgical Press, 1985.

______________. "Chapter II: The Governance of Institutes (cc. 617-640)." In *The Code of Canon Law: A Text and Commentary,* edited by James A. Coriden et al., 475-483. New York/Mahwah: Paulist Press, 1985.

Holland, Sharon. "Internal Governance and Consecrated Life." *CLSA Proceedings* 45 (1983) 37-48.

______________. "Select Questions in Religious Law: Admission, Separation, Approbation." *CLSA Proceedings* 44 (1982) 121-140.

Morrisey, Francis G. "Issues of Confidentiality in Religious Life." *Bulletin on Issues in Religious Law* 4 (1988) 1-10.

McBrien, Richard P. "The Believer's Right to Privacy." In *Privacy: A Vanishing Value?,* edited by William C. Bier, 124-131. New York: Fordham University Press, 1980.

McDermott, Rose. "Chapter III: Admission of Candidates and Formation of Members (cc. 641-661)." In *The Code of Canon*

Law: A Text and Commentary, edited by James A. Coriden et al., 489-499. New York/Mahwah: Paulist Press. 1985.

McManus, Frederick R. "Title IV: The Sacrament of Penance (cc. 959-997)." In *The Code of Canon Law: A Text and Commentary,* edited by James A. Coriden et al., 673-701. New York/Mahwah: Paulist Press, 1985.

Wrenn, Lawrence G. "Title III: The Discipline to be Observed in Tribunals (cc. 1446-1457)." In *The Code of Canon Law: A Text and Commentary,* edited by James A. Coriden et al., 960-966. New York/Mahwah: Paulist Press, 1985.

THE CONFIDENTIALITY OF WRITTEN DOCUMENTS IN CANON LAW

ELISSA A. RINERE, C.P.

The Church has a long history of keeping written records going back, one might say, to the Scriptures. The Church also has a long history of keeping certain things confidential. A clear and consistent example of this is the "seal" of the sacrament of penance. The mixing of these two histories, however, resulting in the confidentiality of written records, doesn't have such a consistent or unequivocal history.

In this study, written documents will be considered in two divisions: non-tribunal documents and tribunal documents. In actual fact, all written records may be considered simply as archives, and a division such as non-tribunal/tribunal is somewhat artificial. For discussing the issue of the confidentiality of written records, however, the division is beneficial.

The basic plan of the study is, first, consideration of non-tribunal documents; that is, parish archives, general diocesan archives, and secret diocesan archives, in the 1917 *Code of Canon Law* and in the current Code. The first section will conclude with some reflections on the canonical protection afforded to these archival materials. The second section of the study will trace the confidentiality of tribunal documents through the major procedural law developments of the twentieth century. Again, the section will conclude with some reflections on the canonical protection afforded to these documents. The tradition being pursued here is, of course, the canonical one; but the need for civil clarifications on confidentiality of ecclesiastical records will be clearly seen.

I. NON-TRIBUNAL DOCUMENTS

A. Parish Archives

All parishes are required to keep written records. The canonical requirements for these records have remained basically the same from the 1917 Code to the revised Code of 1983. According to canon 535 of the latter, each parish is to maintain, at the very least, baptismal, marriage, and death registers.[1] Any notations concerning a person's status in the Church such as adoption, marriage, ordination, or religious profession are to be added to the baptismal register,[2] and these registers are to be kept in a safe place, or archives.[3] A note about access to these registers is made in the last sentence of the canon: "... the pastor is to take care that they do not come into the hands of outsiders."[4] Although one commentator[5] mentions the care which should be taken with delicate information, such as that concerning a person's adoptive background, the law does not clearly allow the possibility of withholding such information from an individual.[6] Rather, the law states the general principle that individuals may have access to those records which are public in nature and deal with their status in the Church.[7] Public ecclesiastical documents are broadly defined as those which are drawn up by church officials during the exercise of their offices.[8]

[1] c. 535, §1: "Each parish is to possess a set of parish books including baptismal, marriage and death registers as well as other registers prescribed by the conference of bishops or the diocesan bishop; the pastor is to see to it that these registers are accurately inscribed and carefully preserved."

[2] c. 535, §2: "In the baptismal register are also to be noted the person's confirmation and whatever affects the canonical status of the Christian faithful by reason of marriage, ..., adoption, reception of sacred orders, perpetual profession in a religious institute, and change of rite; these notations are always to be noted on a document which certifies the reception of baptism."

[3] c. 535, §4: "Each parish is to have a registry or archive in which the parish books are kept along with episcopal letters and other documents which ought to be preserved due to necessity or usefulness..."

[4] "... parochus caveat ne ad extraneorum manus perveniant." By analogy with *Provida Mater* to be discussed below, one could conclude that "outsiders" are those persons who would misuse the information available in archival documents, especially in civil litigation.

[5] John Alesandro, "The Internal Ordering of Particular Churches (cc. 431-459)," in Coriden, James, et al., eds., *The Code of Canon Law: A Text and Commentary* (New York/Mahwah: Paulist Press, 1985) p. 430 (Hereafter cited as *Commentary*).

[6] Certainly, most adoptive agencies have their own policies on the release or nonrelease of such background information, but parishes are sometimes in possession of this material and have been known to act independently.

[7] c. 487, §2: "It is a right of interested parties to obtain personally or through their proxy an authentic written copy or a photocopy of documents which are public by their nature and which pertain to the status of such persons."

[8] c. 1540, §1: "Public ecclesiastical documents are those which official persons have drawn up in the exercise of their function in the Church, after having observed the formalities prescribed by law."

This stance on availability of public documents has been consistent in both codes. The 1917 Code provided for access to archival material by "interested parties," and the possibility of these parties being given legal copies of documents.[9] the revised Code restates this provision and emphasizes it by calling access to public records on ecclesiastical status a "right" of the party concerned.[10]

This right is qualified, of course. The interpretation of canon 487, §2 must be balanced by an individual's right of privacy, the right to one's good name, and the obligation of Church officials to be responsible in the administration of their duties.[11] In practice, on the parish level, it is often left to the judgment of the pastor or other parish representatives to balance these rights and obligations in individual cases.

In 1980 the American Diocesan Archivists addressed this issue of access to sacramental records in a memo directed to the canonical affairs committee of the NCCB. The archivists described sacramental records as both public and private in nature. Among their recommendations were the following:

> Access to sacramental records is affected by the passage of time. More recent records generally require greater restrictions on access than older records.
>
> The example of the United States Census Bureau should be followed by using the year 1900 as a cut-off date in granting access to sacramental records. Records before that date may be broadly available to researchers; records after that date should be restricted from use.
>
> After preliminary legal study of the national level by the NCCB, each diocese should establish a specific policy on access to sacramental records in light of its local situation, the appropriate state laws regarding

[9]1917 CIC, c. 384, §1.

[10]See note 7, "It is a *right . . .*"

[11]For comments on the balancing of these elements, see, for instance Edward Dillon, "Confidentiality of Ecclesiastical Records," *The Catholic Lawyer* 30 (1986) 177-197. Also, see Francis Morrisey, "Issues of Confidentiality in Religious Life," *Bulletin on Issues in Religious Law*, vol. 4, n.1, April 1988.

privacy, and after a wide, inclusive consultation with a number of individuals and groups.[12]

B. Diocesan Archives

1. General Archives

On the diocesan level, the law also requires record keeping. The 1917 Code contained a fairly detailed section on diocesan archives, both general and secret, but did not stipulate specifically which records were to be kept.[13] Generally, the diocesan archives were to be kept under lock and key. They were available for reference only through permission from the diocesan bishop, or from the vicar general and the chancellor.[14] The chancellor was the chief archivist and only holder of the key.[15] With permission, documents could be signed out of the archives for three days at a time and extensions were not to be easily given.[16]

The 1983 Code simplifies many of the requirements for diocesan archives made in the earlier Code. Keys are to be in possession of the diocesan bishop as well as the chancellor.[17] Permission to go into the archives is obtained from the bishop or from the moderator of the curia *and* the chancellor.[18] Documents can be removed from the archives for an unspecified period of time with the permission of these same individuals.[19] The general right of access to public documents for interested persons, as stated above, is clear from canon 487, §2, with the necessity of balancing rights kept in mind.

In recent years issues associated with diocesan archives have been the subject of much discussion. The issues are theoretically complementary to provisions of the law, but, in fact, they seem

[12]Unpublished memo dated November 1, 1980. The cited statements are from the section of the memo entitled "Recommendations on Access and Use of Sacramental Records."

[13]The public ecclesiastical documents identified in c. 1813 of the 1917 Code are, in practice, the basic general archival elements: documents issued by Ordinaries in the exercise of their office, those signed by ecclesiastical notaries, judicial ecclesiastical records, and sacramental registers.

[14]1917 CIC, c. 377.

[15]1917 CIC, cc. 372 and 377.

[16]1917 CIC, c. 378.

[17]c. 487.

[18]Ibid.

[19]c. 488.

to be an attempt to provide for certain *lacunae*. For instance, diocesan archives are acknowledged as the key to the accurate history of a local church. Bishops have been urged to employ professional archivists and to make diocesan archives available to researchers and historians.

> ... no bishop need fear that by opening his archives to scholarly examination, he will expose the Church's past to deliberate attempts at embarrassment. True, scandals and shortcomings may be uncovered, but in these matters we believe it is still appropriate to follow the admonition of Pope Leo XIII... 'that the first law of history is not to dare to utter falsehood; the second, not to fear to speak the truth; and, moreover, no room must be left for suspicion of partiality or prejudice.'[20]

In 1978 the Secretariat of State of the Vatican issued guidelines on the microfilming of documents in ecclesiastical archives.[21] Among the norms is one stipulating that archival material which is not confidential or secret in nature should be made available for research only after seventy years.[22] Decisions to release private or confidential documents are not to be made without consultation with individuals, families, or organizations concerned.[23]

Thus, the law is somewhat ambiguous on the point of access to archives. Policy statements from various sources support both the conflicting values of confidentiality and access. In the practical realm there are still unanswered questions. As a result of this situation, dioceses would be well advised to take the initiative and apply to general diocesan archives the recommendation cited above in reference to sacramental records. With diocesan legislation, practice should be consistent through the diocese and the legislation would serve as a canonical protection against civil challenges which the universal law does not clearly provide.

[20] National Conference of Catholic Bishops, "A Document on Ecclesiastical Archives," November 22, 1974.

[21] The norms were communicated to Archbishop John Quinn, President of the NCCB, by Archbishop Jean Jadot, Apostolic Delegate, in a letter dated August 4, 1978.

[22] This is in keeping with the policy established in 1881 by the Vatican Secret Archives. A new section of this archives is opened every ten years.

[23] Norm 3 of the memo.

2. Secret Archives

In very broad canonical terms, documents which are "public in nature" deal with matters of the external forum. That is, they document matters which are tangible and observable. These public documents are distinct from those which pertain to matters of conscience, or the internal forum. These latter are secret and are kept in the diocesan secret archives. This secret file is said to have originated in law in 1741 by decree of Pope Benedict XIV. Its first purpose was to secure documentation on secret marriages.[24]

The 1917 Code provided that the secret archives were locked at all times. Under ordinary circumstances they were available only to the diocesan bishop or, when the see was vacant, to the apostolic administrator.[25] Two keys were required to open the secret archives. One was in the possession of the diocesan bishop and the other was held by the vicar general or the chancellor.[26] Other canons gave very specific instructions on the possession and use of the keys when the see was vacant or otherwise impeded.[27] Certainly, the expectation was that documents in the secret archives were not available.

The revised Code simplifies many elements of the "key" provisions for the secret archives but maintains the high degree of confidentiality surrounding them and it places even stricter limits on access. Only the bishop is to have a key to this file. When the see is vacant, the secret archives are opened only "in a case of true necessity" and only by the diocesan administrator. The prohibition against removing documents from the secret archives is unqualified.[28]

Among the documents to be kept in these secret archives are:

[24]Francisco Wernz, and Petri Vidal, *Ius Canonicum* (Romae: Pontificia Universitas Gregoriana, 1943) 2:218.

[25]1917 CIC, c. 379, §3, §4.

[26]Ibid.

[27]1917 CIC, cc. 380, 381, 382.

[28]c. 490, §1: "Only the bishop may have the key to the secret archive.

§2: When the see is vacant the secret archive or safe is not to be opened, except in a case of true necessity by the diocesan administrator himself.

§3: Documents are not to be removed from the secret archive or safe."

a) acts of criminal cases which concern matters of morals,[29] b) matrimonial dispensations in the non-sacramental internal forum, c) the register for secret marriages, d) dispensations from impediments and irregularities to orders, e) decrees of dismissal from religious institutes, and f) documents relating to the loss of the clerical state by invalidity, penalty, or dispensation.[30]

But this list is not exhaustive. An individual bishop is free to place other documents or information into these secret archives to lessen or prevent the possibility of scandal or damage to someone's good name.[31] Such documents could conceivably include personnel records or psychiatric reports, and the like. Canonically, once placed in the secret archives, these documents would be secure and confidential. In fact, it can be said that at its root, the intent of the law with respect to these secret archives is that in the world of facts and documentation–the external forum–the secret archives do not exist.

The strict confidentiality given to the secret archives in canon law is a protection in civil law, but it does not necessarily lead to civilly protected confidentiality.[32] It has been suggested that the provisions of canon 489, §1 on the periodic destruction of the acts of criminal cases be adapted and applied to any "documentation that could be derogatory to a person's reputation," and that such materials be kept only as long as is necessary.[33] Also, invoking the value of particular law, diocesan statutes on the content and status of documents placed in the secret archives would be a further protection.

[29]This is stipulated in c. 489, §2. The canon also provides that such documents are to be destroyed when the criminal has died, or when ten years have passed since the penalty was inflicted. The only information to be retained in the secret archives is a brief summary of the case and the text of the definitive sentence.

Also, it should be noted that the "acts of criminal cases which concern matters of morals" are, in fact, tribunal documents. However, the remanding of these acts to the secret archives surrounds them with a degree of confidentiality different from that afforded to other tribunal documents.

[30]Alesandro in *Commentary*, p. 397. This listing is unchanged from that given by earlier commentators. See, for instance, Wernz-Vidal 2:820.

[31]Ibid.

[32]David Young, and Steven Tigges, "Discovery and Use of Church Records by Civil Authorities," *The Catholic Lawyer* 30 (1986) 208-209. The authors give some comments, pro and con, on possible appeal to the Free Exercise clause of the U.S. Constitution in order to avoid the disclosure of church documents.

[33]Morrisey, p. 7.

From this it is clear that diocesan officials must be familiar with the civil statutes in their own areas in order to take steps to protect all archives, but especially the secret archives, from subpoena.[34]

II. TRIBUNAL DOCUMENTS

As noted in the introduction, a division between non-tribunal and tribunal documents is being maintained in this study. We now turn attention to tribunal documents; the acts of ecclesiastical trials.

According to canon 1400, §1 of the 1983 *Code of Canon Law,* ecclesiastical trials can have one of three goals: prosecution or vindication of rights, declaration of juridic facts, or the imposition or declaration of penalties. The prosecution or vindication of rights and the declaration of juridic facts are understood in the law as contentious issues. The imposition or declaration of penalties is a criminal or penal process. In theory, all ecclesiastical trials belong either under the first heading or the second. Consideration of the confidentiality of such tribunal records confines discussion primarily to canon 1598 of the revised Code, and to a lesser degree, canon 1554. The former canon treats the requirements for publication of the acts in an ecclesiastical trial. This publication is understood to mean that both parties involved in a trial are given full access to all the evidence collected by the court. The latter canon states the requirements for making known to both parties the names of those persons who have acted as witnesses in a case. To bring to light the canonical issues surrounding the procedural point of publication, its development through the last eighty years will be traced.

A. History of Publication

1. Pre-code Practice

Previous to the promulgation of the 1917 *Code of Canon Law,* the traditional distinction between types of trials was criminal and non-criminal. Generally, the acts of non-criminal cases were published when the parties requested it. The judge, however,

[34]Alesandro in *Commentary,* p. 397.

[35]Lawrence G. Wrenn, in *Commentary,* p. 992.

could deny the request in favor of maintaining confidentiality. Thus, in such cases, publication was not required for the validity of the sentence rendered by the court.[35] In criminal trials, on the other hand, the point was not disputed that publication of the acts was an essential part of the process and needed for the validity of the sentence.

2. The 1917 *Code of Canon Law*

In the 1917 Code the distinction between criminal and non-criminal trials was not maintained. Rather, the Code distinguished between criminal trials and contentious trials. The majority of the procedural canons in this first Code appeared under the heading "Judgments in General," and the content of the canons applied to both kinds of trials. Marriage cases were understood to belong under the heading of contentious trials. The three canons of the 1917 Code to be considered here, canons 1858, 1623 and 1763, appeared under the main heading of "Judgments in General."

The first, canon 1858, provided for the publication of the acts of a case before its discussion and final decision.[36] The two historical texts cited as source material for this canon are from the decretals of Gregory IX.[37] The texts are concerned with ecclesiastical officials, one an abbott and one a ranking prelate, who had been accused of poor administration of funds and simony. In both cases, the proofs collected against the individuals and the names of their accusers had to be made known; that is, the acts had to be published to allow for the preparation of a proper defense. Both these trials would be considered criminal in nature since they involved a determination of guilt or innocence and if the former, the infliction of some ecclesiastical penalty. The preparation of a proper defense, or the right of defense, was understood to be dependent upon the accused having clear and accurate information on what the charges were, and of being able to face accusers at the trial. Thus, in the law governing both contentious and criminal trials, this right of defense presupposed the necessary disclosure of evidence; that

[36] 1917 CIC, c. 1858.

[37] c. 24, X, *de accusationibus, inquisitionibus et denunciationibus,* V, l; c. 31, X *de simonia, et ne aliquid pro spiritualibus exigatur vel promittatur,* V, 3.

is, the publication of the acts.

Canon 1858 did not mention the need for publication of the acts as a condition for the validity of the sentence eventually reached by the court. This omission coupled with the Code's application of the canon to criminal and non-criminal cases alike led to much canonical debate.[38] The majority of commentators held that publication of the acts in any case was required for validity of the proceedings with no distinction made between criminal and contentious trials. They pointed to the relationship between publication of the acts and the right of defense in drawing their conclusions.

This canon on publication must be complemented by canon 1623, §3 which outlined the discretionary power of the judge in a particular case to bind parties and other participants by oaths of secrecy.[39] These oaths were always to be administered in criminal trials and in those contentious trials where there was danger of scandal or damage to reputations. It is interesting to note that all five documents cited in the 1917 Code as sources for this canon originated in the nineteenth century. Three of the documents are concerned with criminal proceedings against clerics,[40] while the other two are concerned with special methods of procedure in marriage cases.[41] Commentators took care to affirm the fact that this discretionary power of the judge was to operate in contentious trials only when planned misuse of the published information was suspected.

To complete the picture presented by the 1917 Code, mention must be made of canon 1763 which stipulated that each party in the case was to be informed of the identity of the witnesses named by the other party. The judge was free to delay this iden-

[38]For a summary of opinions of commentators, see Albert McGoldrick, *Confidentiality of Tribunal Acts: The Civil Law Implications in the USA of Canon 1598, §1*, (Washington, DC: Unpublished licentiate thesis, Catholic University of America, 1986), pp. 7-8.

[39]1917 CIC, c. 1623, §3.

[40]The earliest, dealing with priests accused of moral impropriety, is an instruction issued on February 20, 1866 by the Holy Office. The second is the June 11, 1880 instruction issued by the Congregation for Bishops and Regulars. The third is an 1883 instruction issued by the Congregation for the Propagation of the Faith.

[41]These last two, both issued in 1883, one by the Holy Office and one by the Congregation for the Propagation of the Faith, concern oaths to be administered to witnesses in marriage cases.

tification for a time, but it could not be omitted from the proceedings.[42]

To summarize, the 1917 Code placed requirements for publication of the acts in criminal and contentious trials into the same procedural framework under the heading "Judgments in General." It provided for the publication of all the acts of a case; that is, access by all parties and officers of the court to all the proofs collected. Source material and commentators indicate that a major motivation behind this provision was the protection of the right of defense for the accused party. There was, however, allowance for the exercise of judicial discretion in binding individuals to oaths of secrecy in order to prevent scandal and/or damage to reputations through the misuse of the information. Also, the identity of witnesses named by any one party had to be revealed to the other party. Thus, the right of parties in a trial to know what had been said by whom was considered very important and was well protected.

3. Provida Mater

Previous to the publication of the 1917 Code, procedural law, and specifically that having to do with the processing of marriage cases, had gone through a number of stages of development.[43] In the latest pre-Code stage, the process used by tribunals was a summary process. It was much less rigid than the formal contentious process required in 1917.[44] The Code's new level of universal uniformity presented significant difficulties to tribunals. Also, long before that first Code the processing of marriage cases had become the major work of tribunals. Criminal or other contentious trials were few and far between.

In 1936 the Holy See acknowledged the fact that the general procedures of the Code were problematic. The instruction *Provida Mater*[45] was issued as a complement to the Code to tailor

[42] 1917 CIC, c. 1763.

[43] For a summary of this history see Lawrence G. Wrenn, *Procedures* (Washington, DC: Canon Law Society of America, 1987) pp. 1-9.

[44] Ibid., p. 7.

[45] Congregation for the Discipline of the Sacraments, *Instructio servanda a tribunalibus diocesanis in pertractandia causis de nullitate matrimoniorum*, August 15, 1935: *AAS* 28 (1936) 313-361 (English translation *Canon Law Digest* 2:471-530).

its general procedures to marriage cases specifically.[46] For the purposes of this study, the major adjustment introduced by *Provida Mater* was wider judicial discretion in the matter of maintaining confidentiality. Articles 175, 130, 138, and 184 are pertinent.

Article 175 restated canons 1858 and 1859 of the code with the result that publication of the acts; that is, access to the acts by both parties and their advocates, was held to be the norm for marriage procedures. Article 130, on the other hand, while it did repeat canon 1623, §3 on the freedom of the judge to bind all parties by oaths of secrecy, allowed for the innovation of the judge withholding from the principals in a case the identity of witnesses. The credibility of the witnesses was then to be established through testimonials obtained from third parties. Traditionally, the credibility of witnesses had been established through their acceptability to the principals.

Following on this innovation, article 138 required the publication of these testimonials, unless the judge saw such publication as a threat of grave harm. Completing this adjustment of general procedures for marriage cases, article 184 emphasized the notion that the proofs collected in a marriage case were never to fall into the hands of outsiders. In these three articles, the motive for altering the general procedures was explained as the sensitive nature of the proofs collected in a marriage case.[47] They were seen as essentially different from the proofs collected in other contentious processes, and therefore requiring different protections and considerations. From 1936 on, marriage cases in all ecclesiastical tribunals were heard according to the 1917 Code and *Provida Mater.*

4. The American Procedural Norms

In 1969, thirty-four years after the implementation of *Provida Mater,* the results of a national survey were published by the Canon Law Society of America[48] which documented what most

[46]The introduction to the instruction states: "But experience has shown that the judges of diocesan curiae, when they come to apply the procedural laws, especially the general ones, to particular cases, sometimes encounter difficulties." (Translation taken from *CLD* 2:471.)

[47]William Doheny, *Matrimonial Procedure in Marriage Cases, Volume I Formal Judicial Procedure,* (Milwaukee: Bruce Publishing Co., 1948), pp. 369, 382, and 446.

[48]Michael O'Callaghan, "Regional Tribunals," *Proceedings* (Canon Law Society of America, 1969), p. 147.

tribunal personnel already knew: American tribunals were slow, the process unwieldy, the results of their efforts sparse, and the needs of the people were not being met. A few years previous to this survey, the Society had undertaken a project for procedural law reform and this culminated in the implementation, on July 1, 1970, of a simplified marriage process. The American Procedural Norms (APN)[49] were available to all American tribunals from that date until November 27, 1983 when the revised *Code of Canon Law* came into force.

To trace the issue of confidentiality in the APN, attention must be given to norm 18.

> When, after consultation with the advocate and defender, the judge has decided that all the necessary and available evidence has been obtained, the principals will be permitted to read the acts unless, in the opinion of the judge, there is a danger of the violation of the right of privacy. The judge will consider requests by the principals for further instruction before bringing the case to a conclusion.[50]

This norm expanded the discretionary power of the judge in maintaining confidentiality. The official commentary issued with the norms pointed out that this freedom of the judge to withhold the acts from the parties was to be used sparingly since it was a clear restriction of a right given in the universal law, and only when the secrecy afforded by article 130 of *Provida Mater* did not seem sufficient to obtain the information needed to resolve a particular case. On those occasions norm 18 was intended to serve the cause of truth by freeing witnesses from fear of loss of friendship, embarrassment, or recrimination.[51]

This adjustment from the requirements of the Code and even of *Provida Mater* was well suited to the nature of marriage cases. American tribunals were able to assure confidentiality to witnesses. They were able to reach out to a larger number of petitioners, and to give reasonable assurance that a final deci-

[49]Text and commentary were published in *CLD* 7:950-966.
[50]Ibid., p. 959.
[51]Ibid., p. 960.

sion would be reached.[52] Judicial discretion was seen as a sign of the pastoral orientation of the norms[53] and the norms themselves were described as a procedural law suited to a community rather than to an institution.[54]

Of course, the APN were not without critics.[55] The main objections raised to them, however, were not against practices which had developed around the judicial discretion allowed by norm 18. The objections centered on the issues of competent forum, respect for the rights of respondents, and dispensations from mandatory appeal.[56] In other words, a judge determining to keep evidence confidential and thereby depart from the traditional understanding of publication of the acts was not the problem.

This observation is reinforced by the fact that on March 28, 1971 Pope Paul VI issued an important instruction, *Causas matrimoniales,* dealing with the processing of marriage cases.[57] In it, competent forum, the subject of norm 7 of the APN, was treated, but not the issue of confidentiality or publication of the acts. It should also be noted that *Causas matrimoniales* was presented as the first step in the reform of procedural law for the whole church. The intended reform acknowledged that marriage cases, especially, did not fit into the general procedures provided in universal law.[58] American tribunals were regulated by both the American Procedural Norms and *Causas*

[52]For the results of a "post-APN" survey which documents this increased activity of American tribunals, see Wrenn, Lawrence G., "The American Procedural Norms," *American Ecclesiastical Review* 165 (1971) 175-186.

[53]Thomas J. Green, "The American Procedural Norms–An Assessment," *Studia Canonica* 8 (1974) 326.

[54]Wrenn, "The American Procedural Norms," pp. 178-179.

[55]See for instance, Pericle Felici, "Letter of the Apostolic Signatura–December 14, 1977–P.N. 9597/77," in *The Jurist* 38 (1978) 220-224. The stated motivation for this letter was complaints received by the Signatura about cases processed under the APN.

[56]Felici specifically cited norms 7 and 23 and cited reports of violations of respondent rights stemming from these. The APN themselves (n.22) established the irremediable nullity of a sentence in any case where the right of defense had been denied, but there was (and is) some debate about what this right entails. See below for further comments on the right of defense.

[57]Pope Paul VI, instruction *Causas matrimoniales,* March 28, 1971: *AAS* 63 (1971) 441-446.

[58]The introduction to the instruction states: "Therefore, while awaiting the fuller reform of the marriage process which our Commission for the Revision of the Code of Canon Law is preparing, we thought it well to issue certain norms on the constitution of ecclesiastical tribunals and on the judicial process, which will expedite the matrimonial process itself." (Trans. taken from *CLD* 7:975.)

matrimoniales until the revised *Code of Canon Law* went into effect on November 27, 1983.

B. *The Revision Process*

After operating for some time under the interim documents treated above, American tribunal personnel were quite surprised to read in the 1976 schema on procedural law:

> Canon 257, §1: Before the discussion of the case all proofs which are in the acts and up to this point have remained secret, are, under pain of nullity, to be published.[59]

With the addition of the phrase "under pain of nullity," the canon added new inflexibility to canon 1858 of the 1917 code. Thus, it was more than a return to the past. The added phrase was a clear departure from the practices which had developed in tribunals under *Provida Causas,* and the APN. The proposed text was termed "disastrous"[60] for tribunals and pleas were made for modifications and changes.[61] One major argument in favor of adjustment of the proposed canon was the possibility for civil litigation which would arise from publication of the acts of a marriage case.[62] The debate was overtly over a point of procedure; but given the history of the question, it can be concluded that the underlying debate really concerned the nature of the marriage process vis-a-vis the ordinary contentious process.[63]

[59]Pontificia Commissio Codici Iuris Canonici Recognoscendo, *Schema canonicum de modo procedendi pro tutela iurium seu De Processibus,* (Romae: Typis Polyglottis Vaticanis, 1976).

[60]Canon Law Society of America, "Report of a Special Committee of the Task Force of the C.L.S.A. on the *Schema canonum de modo procendi pro tutela iurium seu De Processibus,* (1977) pp. 3-11 sets out the reasons behind this description.

[61]The Canon Law Society of Great Britain and Ireland, for instance, basing its argument on the "laws of charity," requested a provision through which the judge could withhold the acts of a marriage case from the parties while making them available to the advocates. See McGoldrick, p. 23 for exact citations.

[62]This point on civil litigation was made by the Canon Law Society of America, the Canon Law Society of Great Britain and Ireland, the Canon Law Society of Australia and New Zealand, and the faculty of St. Paul's University, Ottawa, Canada. See McGoldrick, pp. 17-19 for specific citations.

[63]The presence of this underlying debate is made clear in the CLSA critique although publication of the acts is not one of the specific issues addressed. For instance: "The Schema presupposes that marriage cases involve a conflict of rights and/or civil consequences. That is not our American experience. Marriage cases are generally inquiries about the validity of marriages in order to clarify ecclesial status." (p. 2)

Through the remainder of the revision process the debate continued. In its 1978 meeting, the coetus dealing with procedural law reinstated the principle of judicial discretion which had been stated in *Provida Mater.*[64] In order to avoid a grave danger the judge could determine to show certain acts *(aliquod actum)* to no one. This reformulation implicitly recognized, as *Provida* had, that differences do exist between cases which the law groups together under the heading of "contentious." The major stated motive behind the reformulation was the possibility of civil litigation if all the acts of a marriage case were published.[65]

The 1980 Schema repeated the revised 1978 text almost verbatim. Although it was acknowledged as an improvement, the canon was still subjected to wide criticism. A major difficulty remained the civil consequences of publication and the necessity of publication "under pain of nullity of the sentence." Alterations of the text were suggested by various members of the Code Commission, but none were accepted. The coetus responded that the proposed text was sufficient, and since publication of the acts was closely related to the right of defense the general principle could not be changed.[66]

C. *The 1983 Code of Canon Law*

In 1982 a second schema of the revised Code was issued. The canon on publication, now canon 1598, §1 remains unchanged in the promulgated 1983 Code.

> c. 1598, §1: After the proofs have been collected the judge by a decree must, under pain of nullity, permit the parties and their advocates to inspect at the tribunal chancery the acts which are not yet known to

[64]*Communicationes* 11 (1979) 135 records the proposed text: "Acquisitis probationibus, iudex decreto partibus et eorum advocatis permittere debet, sub poena nullitatis, ut acta nondum eis nota apud Tribunalis cancellariam inspiciant; quin etiam advocatis id petentibus dari potest actorum exemplar, nisi in causis ad bonum publicum spectantibus iudex ad gravissima pericula evitanda aliquod actum nemini tradendum esse censeat."

[65]Ibid., p. 134.

[66]*Relatio complectens synthesim animadversionem ab em.mis atque exc.mis patribus commisionis ad novissimum schema codici iuris canonici exhibitarum, cum responsibus a secretaria et consultoribus datis* (Romae: Typis Polyglottis Vaticanis, 1981), p. 323.

> them; a copy of the acts can also be given to advocates upon request; however, in cases concerned with the public good, in order to avoid very serious dangers, the judge can decree that a given act is not to be shown to anyone, with due concern, however, that the right of defense always remains intact.

The addition of that final clause to the text of the canon is unexplained in the official records of the revision process.

From the text, however, it can be inferred that again special procedural allowances were made for marriage cases apart from other contentious trials. Certainly, the danger of civil litigations arising from publication was a factor in the development of the canon, but the nature of the marriage case itself had to have been considered, at least indirectly.

Before proceeding to some comments on canon 1598, the final point in the 1983 Code to be considered here is canon 1554. In it the law requires, as did the 1917 Code, that the identity of all witnesses be made known to the parties.[67] This provision did not go through extensive evolution or debate in the revision process despite its departure from *Provida Mater* which permitted exceptions to the general rule. The present law allows for no exceptions in this matter of the making known the identity of witnesses.[68]

In summary, for tribunal documents the 1983 Code presents publication as the norm, but then allows for moderation of that right as long as the right of defense remains intact. It is the nature of the case under consideration which determines how these rights are to be balanced.

D. Interpretation of Canon 1598, §1

The provisions of canon 1598 apply to both criminal and contentious trials. The general rule of the first paragraph applies to

[67]c. 1554: "Before witnesses are examined, their names are to be made known to the parties; however, if in the prudent assessment of the judge, that cannot be done without serious difficulty, it is to be done at least before the publication of the testimony."

[68]See cc. 1547-1573 for the laws governing witnesses and their testimony. It should be noted that many tribunals, because of personnel and time constraints, do not call witnesses to give formal testimony in marriage cases. Rather, they receive written statements or affidavits from the persons named. The affidavits then become part of the acts and are subject to the provisions of c. 1598.

criminal trials. The parties and their advocates must be permitted to inspect the acts of the case. This is an important provision since, in a criminal trial the defendant has been accused of some crime, and only through access to the acts can that person prepare a proper defense.

The general rule does not apply, and the situation is not so clear, in cases involving the public good, of which marriage cases are one example. In such instances, the judge may depart from the general rule "in order to avoid a most serious danger." It is the responsibility of the judge to identify and determine the severity of the danger. Possibilities include dissension, scandal, or the endangerment of someone's reputation.[69] Then, by decree, certain acts are excluded from publication.[70] These excluded documents may be seen by officials of the court, but not by the parties themselves.[71]

The last point in the canon, the inviolability of the right of defense in any moderation of the right to know, raises a few difficulties since the actual meaning of the "right of defense" in marriage cases is a point of debate. Beneath this specific debate on the right of defense is the larger and pervasive debate on the true nature of the marriage case. A few words on this specific debate will help to clarify the larger issue.

Concerning the right of defense, one view states that in a marriage case "the issue is not the good name of either party but the validity of the marriage bond."[72] Built on this foundation, the right of defense is said to belong to the individual in the trial whose primary concern is that bond; that is, the right of defense belongs primarily to the Defender of the Bond, and not necessarily to the respondent.[73] Consequently, and especially when the presence of any contention whatsoever is low, certain acts can be withheld from publication while the right of defense remains intact. A high

[69]Wrenn in *Commentary*, p. 992.

[70]*Ibid.*, p. 992. The author notes that the phrase *aliquod actum* refers to the freedom of the judge to decree the exclusion of a particular document from publication or the exclusion of certain categories of documents, such as the reports of experts.

[71]Ibid.

[72]Ibid., p. 992.

[73]Ibid. Wrenn cites, as a source for this view, *Dei miseratione*, issued in 1741 by Benedict XIV. He also cites a Rotal decision *coram* Brennan, of November 27, 1958, in which this understanding of the right of defense is explicitly stated.

degree of confidentiality maintained in such a framework of interpretation is canonically protected. The right to know and the right of defense are separable.

In a differing view, it is put forward that in a marriage case the right of defense belongs primarily to the person of the respondent who has been called upon to answer certain accusations of wrong-doing, or who, it is presumed, wishes to argue against the nullity of marriage. Thus,

> once the preparatory phase (of the case) has been completed, both parties, that is the respondent as well, must be given the opportunity to examine all of the matter gathered. This is under sanction of nullity (c. 1598, §1).[74]

Here, the right to know and the right of defense do not appear to be separable. Under such an interpretation, a high degree of confidentiality for tribunal acts would not be well protected canonically.

These differing views are predicated upon the broader issue of the nature of the marriage case itself. Since 1917 canon law has classified the processing of marriage cases as ordinary contentious trials; that is, as disputed issues. However, history shows that the law's requirements for publication of the acts in ordinary contentious trials simply did not "work" for tribunals. This led to adjustments of the general process through *Provida Mater,* and then, for American tribunals, the APN. The special character of marriage cases was accommodated in these procedural law changes. The smooth and fruitful operation which American tribunals experienced under the APN highlights this fact. But confidentiality is only one point in the ordinary contentious process that doesn't "work" for marriage cases. A listing of the ill-suited points, would wisely begin with the very name "contentious."

> That marriage cases should automatically be considered contentious is itself a contentious matter... Many American and other canonists have contended for years that those marriage cases in which neither the respondent nor the defender opposes an annulment should be considered, not as contentious, but simply

[74]Zenon Grocholewski, "Current Questions Concerning the State and Activity of Tribunals With Particular Reference to the United States of America," in *Incapacity for Marriage: Jurisprudence and Interpretation* (Rome: Gregorian University, 1987), p. 252.

as declarative of a person's official status in the Catholic community.[75]

The root of the problem at hand is not, therefore, the isolated procedural point of publication, but the pervasive question of the true nature of the "non-contentious" (or undisputed) marriage case.[76] Just as with the right of defense, canonical interpretation of the law on publication *vs.* confidentiality will differ depending on the interpreter's view of the marriage case itself as a clearly contentious issue or a non-contentious process whose purpose is to clarify an individual's marital status in the Church.

E. Conclusion

Once a marriage case is completed, the acts become part of the general diocesan archives. Canonical protection of the confidentiality of these archives was discussed earlier. What would happen, however, if a respondent, not necessarily hostile but simply curious, challenged the level of confidentiality established by the judge and wanted access to some of, if not all, the evidence which remained unpublished from the trial?

A first level of protection would be that claimed for general archival material. Additional canonical protection would be afforded to the marriage case through the decree of the judge as called for in canon 1598, §1, presuming that the decree is drawn up properly. But ultimately, the question will have to be addressed of what the acts of the case are actually documenting. Do they pertain to a contentious trial in fact or merely in theory?

If they document a trial which is contentious *in fact,* then maybe respondents, even though not hostile, should have their curiosity satisfied. If there have been accusations and wrongdoing has been imputed, then a person has a right to know these things and to refute the charges.

If the acts document a trial which is contentious only in theory, then what is it, *in fact*? The hypothetical problem of what to do about the curious respondent, not to mention the hostile respondent, won't be answered until that question is answered. Canonical debate over the proper level of confidentiality to be maintained for tribunal documents won't be settled until then either.

[75]Wrenn in *Commentary,* p. 948.

[76]*Ibid.* "This is not merely a semantic problem, but an important question of taxonomy."

Grounding the "Priest-Penitent Privilege" in American Law

RONALD P. STAKE

It is widely held that no privilege of confidential communication between a priest and penitent existed in English common law.[1] Upon this view one constructs a legal basis for the privilege by looking to the legislation of a particular state rather than to a common legal heritage based on reason. Statutes determine the existence and scope of the privilege. This is a straight forward and positivistic approach to grounding the priest-penitent privilege in the civil law.

There is another and more philosophical approach. It is possible to look to the development of practice and doctrine to find reasons for articulating the priest-penitent privilege within the framework of the free exercise of religion.[2] Here the discussion treats the general development of the *seal of confession.*[3] The seal of confession, however, is a limited concept, and it was articulated relatively late in the history of Christianity. Behind the seal are older values connected to the pastoral care of souls, and these can be exploited to ground a privilege beyond the confessional forum and in fundamental constitutional law.

1. *Development of Sacramental Confession and the Seal*

In 1967 an encyclopedia article on the seal of confession contained the following sentence:

> (I)t was accepted from the beginning that the penitent has some right to secrecy and that this right and

[1]See 8 Wigmore, *Evidence* §2394 (McNaughton rev. ed., 1961).

[2]U.S. Const., amend. 1: "Congress shall make no law respecting the establishment of religion, or prohibiting the free exercise thereof..."

[3]See 1983 *CIC,* cc. 983, 984, 1388; *Rite of Penance,* n. 10d.

> the corresponding obligation on the part of the confessor are a natural concomitant of the divine command to confess.[4]

To support this statement the author of the article refers to the Council of Trent.[5] There are problems with the statement from the perspective of history. First, the statement presupposes a sacramental practice of medieval origin as one "existing from the beginning." Second, the concept of a *right* as something possessed by an individual is a modern idea.[6] Third, *secrecy* as a domain of personal integrity is also a modern idea.[7] Finally, the reference to the "divine command to confess" is problematic if one takes this uncritically to mean sacramental confession of sins to a priest.[8]

Scholarship in this century has retrieved a very fluid picture of the development of the Christian Church's practice of sacramental reconciliation. James Dallen's *The Reconciling Community: The Rite of Penance*[9] traces this development through three overlapping periods: ancient penance (first six centuries), medieval penance (seventh through 15th centuries), and modern penance (16th century and after). Dallen's view is that the sacrament of penance has been practiced in a variety of forms and has as its principal objective the restoration of sinners to the Church and Eucharist. Through personal and serious sin baptized Christians disrupt communion with the Church and separate themselves from the visible Body of Christ. This cuts one off from external participation in that community that receives and celebrates Christ's good news of salvation. Sacramental penance forgives sins and reconciles one with God because it restores one to communion with the Church.

[4]J.L. McCarthy, "Confession, Seal of," 4 *New Catholic Encyclopedia* 133 (1967).

[5]See Denz 1707: "Any one who says that the secret manner of confession to the priest alone–which the Church has always observed and still observes– is alien to the institution and command of Christ and is a human invention" is anathema.

[6]See, e.g., R. Dworkin, *Taking Rights Seriously* (1977); D. Hollenbach, *Claims in Conflict: Retrieving and Renewing the Catholic Human Rights Tradition* (1979).

[7]For a detailed analysis of the concept of secrecy see S. Bok, *Secrets: On the Ethics of Concealment and Revelation* (1983).

[8]The only clear injunction the New Testament contains concerning the confession of sins is James 5: 16: "So confess your sins to one another, and pray for one another, and this will cure you; the heartfelt prayer of a good man works very powerfully." The passage is not a reference to sacramental confession.

[9]J. Dallen, *The Reconciling Community: The Rite of Penance* (1986).

From this view of the sacrament one can appreciate the ancient practices that excommunicated serious sinners and restored them to participation in the Eucharist. The ancient ritual was public, and like the catechumenate process through which new Christians were formed and welcomed the liturgy of penance and reconciliation was a long process presided over by the bishop. Sins that were public and threatening to the body of the Church were reserved to this public liturgy. Among the sins reserved were apostasy, murder, and adultery. Other and less serious sins were experienced as forgiven through individual works of charity, through prayer, and, above all, in the very celebration of the Eucharist. Throughout the first six centuries and for much of the medieval period the private confession of sins to a priest was not part of the Church's sacrament of reconciliation.[10]

A confession was part of the ancient discipline, but this was the *exomologesis,* not so much an admission of sins as a confession of faith:

> *Exomologesis* acknowledges God's greatness, a greatness shown through mercy leading sinners to repentence, and breathes the same spiritual atmosphere as the Jewish *berakoth.* It is not primarily the acknowledgment of sins–this took place through presenting oneself publicly as a penitent–but rather a confession of faith, the praise of God, and an appeal for the community's prayerful support. This outlook characterizes the liturgies of penance and reconciliation throughout the ancient period.[11]

Beginning in the fourth century a form of the care of souls that we would today recognize as spiritual direction appeared in the Christian Churches of the East. This ministry of the desert fathers, monks, and others assisted individual Christians in living lives more fully under the influence of the Gospel.[12] Such spiritual direction was a freely chosen and non-sacramental practice. Recourse to spiritual directors would entail the disclosure of one's secrets,

[10]*Id.* at 66-67.
[11]*Id. at 32-33.*
[12]See K. Leech, *Soul Friend: The Practice of Christian Spirituality* (1977).

including "confessional matter" in the modern sense of the term. In these encounters freedom was valued and the character of *discretion* was always to be exercised by those who were the spiritual directors.[13] Early spiritual direction and its later developments in the West were linked to the sacrament of penance, but only accidentally. Individuals could choose the path of spiritual direction as a way of discerning whether or not to enter the public discipline of the sacrament.[14]

Among the ancient Celtic churches of the British Isles the public liturgy of penance never took root. By the time these churches were flourishing the public celebrations of the sacrament of penance were already on the decline everywhere. In Ireland monastic influence became the major force in the popular spirituality. Adapting the Eastern practices of spiritual direction the Irish monks extended this ministry to persons living near the monasteries. By the sixth century a type of spiritual direction developed there which entailed the confession of sins. Later practice would focus almost exclusively on such confessions. Throughout the middle ages this type of confession-focused spiritual direction-spread across Europe through the influence of the *penitentials*, practical manuals prescribing penitential works as tariffs or commutations in respect to sins of various kinds and

[13]*Discretion* was not only viewed in the modern sense of having the ability to be discreet, it encompasses the entire realm of the concern a pastor has for a member of the church:

> The disciples also looked to these men for *discretion*. This virtue was seen as the essential feature of the true spiritual master from the time of St. Anthony the Great onwards. The spiritual director was not simply someone who taught a spiritual technique, but he was a father who helped to shape the inner life of his sons through his prayer, concern and pastoral care. One sees the place of the spiritual father clearly in the Apophthegmata or Sayings of the Desert Fathers. Here one meets the figure of the *abba*, the charismatic holy man of the wilderness, and the sayings of these men contain answers to practical problems and difficulties.

K. Leech, *Soul Friend* at 41-42. Throughout the Sayings is evidence of care taken to protect the secrets of those who came to the *abbas* for direction. An example of this:

> They said of abba Macarius that he became as it is written a god upon earth, because just as God protects the world, so abba Macarius would cover the faults that he saw as though he did not see them, and those which he heard as though he did not hear them.

"The living Spirit," 6 Aug. 1988 *The Tablet* 914, quoting *The Desert of the Heart: Daily Readings with the Desert Fathers* (B. Ward ed. 1988).

[14]See Dallen, *The Reconciling Community* at 44-45, 66-67.

degrees. The emphasis was no longer the public support of sinners seeking restoration to communion with the Church. Instead, confession of sins and penances were viewed as a private arena where sinners sought forgiveness in ways parallel to the payment of debts and the satisfaction of wrongs in Celtic law. This practice was not originally a substitute for the sacrament's public liturgy; it developed out of spiritual direction and sacramental absolution was not involved.

The people experienced consolation and forgiveness through these private encounters with monks and ordinary priests who took up the practice as its value became indisputable. A long struggle took place before this style of ministry would supplant the public liturgies of reconciliation and receive episcopal sanction. Compared to the lengthy and difficult penances of the public and canonical form of the sacrament, the ease of the private forum and its tariff penances, later reduced to a formula of prayer or pious work, was received well and eventually recognized as a legitimate form of the sacrament. By the 12th century it was the only form of the sacrament of penance that had a living reality within the Western Church. Within this development the notion of the seal of confession arose and became part of the canonical ordering of the sacrament.[15] At the Fourth Lateran Council in 1215 the confession of one's sins to the priest was mandated as an annual obligation for those in serious sin, and the obligation of the seal was universally imposed upon all confessors.[16] From Lateran IV the seal of confession has been retained through the centuries and included in the recent revision of the *Code of Canon Law*:

[15]Clear references to confessional secrecy begin appearing in the ninth century at the local level (Council of Douzy in 874); Gratian's *Decretum* includes the concept that would later be called the "seal": "Let the priest who dares to make known the sins of his penitent be disposed." (*CorpIurCan*DePoen D.6, c.2).

[16]Fourth Lateran Council, c. 21 (1215):

> Let the priest absolutely beware that he does not by word or sign or by any manner whatever in any way betray the sinner: but if he should happen to need wiser counsel let him cautiously seek the same without any mention of the person. For whoever shall dare to reveal a sin disclosed to him in the tribunal of penance we decree that he shall be not only deposed from the priestly office but that he shall also be sent into the confinement of a monastery to do perpetual penance.

R.S. Nolan, "Seal of Confession," 13 *Catholic Encyclopedia* 649 (1912).

> Canon 983, §1. The sacramental seal is inviolable; therefore, it is a crime for a confessor in any way to betray a penitent by word or in any other manner or for any reason.
>
> §2. An interpreter, if there is one present, is also obliged to preserve the secret, and also all others to whom knowledge of sins from confession shall come in any way.
>
> Canon 984, §1. Even if every danger of revelation is excluded, a confessor is absolutely forbidden to use knowledge acquired from confession when it might harm the penitent.
>
> §2. One who is placed in authority can in no way use for external governance knowledge about sins which he has received in confession at any time.
>
> Canon 1388, §1. A confessor who directly violates the seal of confession incurs an automatic *(latae sententiae)* excommunication reserved to the Apostolic See; if he does so only indirectly, he is to be punished in accord with the seriousness of the offense.
>
> §2. An interpreter and other persons mentioned in canon 983, §2, who violate this secrecy are to be punished with a just penalty, not excluding excommunication.[17]

The seal of confession is a necessary adjunct to the canonical ordering of private penance. Once the confession of sins is demanded as an integral part of the sacrament the seal must follow. What discretion requires of those who received the freely given secrets from others in the forum of spiritual direction, the law now requires of the priest to whom sins are confessed under obligation. So, the protection of the seal is not simply an instrumental encouragement to get people to confess; it is a duty on the part of the Church in representation of God who reconciles sinners in Christ without revealing their secrets, without harming them in any way.[18]

[17]1983 *CIC,* cc. 983, 984, 1388.

[18]The image of "covering faults" that appears in the description of abba Macarius in note 13, *supra,* stems from the Christian conviction that God does not hold our sins against us, that he blots them out. This is the Father-God portrayed in the parable of the Prodigal Son, Luke 15: 11-32.

Dallen ascribes significance to the seal of confession in a brief reference. Confidentiality within the sacramental forum concerns the confessor's role in the discernment of spirits. This is the critical and essential element in spiritual direction, the end toward which the character of discretion was employed. Discernment is also critical in the process of the evangelization of conscience.[19] What the present rituals of penance seek is free response to the power of the Gospel. In an atmosphere of prayerful dialogue the confession of one's sins manifests a willingness on the part of a penitent to hear the Gospel, submit to it, and change one's life (conversion). The seal not only helps to promote this atmosphere, but it is essential for the existence of the atmosphere lest one be fearful of and preoccupied by judgment rather than be involved in prayer and worship:

> By associating discernment of spirits with the judicial role, that of presiding, the RP seeks to ensure that spiritual counsel is always subordinate to worship and that instruction is not to the detriment of prayer but part of sharing the Word. The requirement of the seal–absolute confidentiality concerning anything that would be to the penitent's disadvantage–is seen in this same context (RP 10d).[20]

2. *The Status of the Seal of Confession in English Law*

There is clear evidence that at least from the Fourth Lateran Council the seal of confession was received and enforced by the ecclesiastical law of the Catholic Church in England.[21] The case is not so clear that confessional secrecy was accepted as an evidentiary privilege in the royal courts and received into the common law of the realm. Written evidence concerning the status of the seal in the secular courts is lacking for the whole period prior to the Reformation.

Some of the decrees of Lateran IV were accepted by the common law courts,[22] and one might assume that the decree con-

[19]The term "evangelization of conscience" entails the power of the Gospel to reveal to an individual the fact and the seriousness of one's own sins.

[20]Dallen, *The Reconciling Community* at 310.

[21]See Nolan, "Seal of Confession" at 649-650.

[22]*Id.* at 651.

cerning the obligation of the seal was also accepted. However, constant rivalry between the royal and ecclesiastical jurisdictions in England prevents one from making too much of an argument from the specifics of one case to those of another. The best case for the seal of confession having been received into the common law is the one that can be made purely on the basis of silence.

The argument from silence presupposes the issue to have arisen in the pre-Reformation era. An attempt to deny benefit of the seal would certainly have provoked instant objection, one that would have left its mark on the recorded history of England.

> The fact that the laws of the Church were so emphatic on the subject, coupled with the fact that the Church was then the Church of the nation, affords good ground for inferring that the secular courts recognized the seal. The recognition of it would not have rested on any principle of immunity from disclosure of confidential communications made to clergymen. It would have rested on the fact that confession was a sacrament, on the fact of that necessity for it which the doctrine of the Church laid down, on the fact of the practice of it by both king and people, and on the fact that the practice was wholly a matter of spiritual discipline and one, moreover, in regard to which the Church had so definitely declared the law of absolute secrecy.[23]

The presupposition that the issue was brought into the courts, however, is itself not clearly evident. It is just as likely, if not more so, that the matter never came up. This is even more probable because of the situation of evidentiary rules that prevailed even through the Reformation times and well into the modern era. No reason to address the issue of the seal while the law permitted torture for the extraction of confessions and officials allowed tainted evidence and perjury when expedience or policy required it.

The first clear reference to the seal of confession in an English trial appears in the first years of the reign of James I. This is well after the Reformation was consolidated in the long reign of

[23]*Id.* at 650.

Elizabeth I. The case was the trial of the superior of the English Jesuits, Father Henry Garnet, for his role in the Gunpowder Plot. At issue was not Fr. Garnet's refusal to give evidence but his knowledge of the facts surrounding the attempted conspiracy to blow up the houses of Parliament in 1605.[24] The defense conjectured that *if* Garnet had knowledge of the plot he had heard the facts only through confession in the sacrament of penance and that the seal of confession would have prohibited disclosure of the facts to the authorities. Whatever the truth, the court's members treated the defense seriously.[25]

Lord Salisbury attempted to demonstrate that the facts of the plot were known to Fr. Garnet through means outside the protection of the seal. [26] Sir Edward Coke, later Lord Chief Justice of England, argued the case for the prosecution. He made a number of points: the confession was not sacramental; Fr. Garnet learned of the plot outside the sacramental forum; the common law did not recognize the obligation of the seal of confession in cases of high treason.[27] This last point implies some recognition that the common law accepted the seal in ordinary trials for felonies. Nonetheless, the case seems to have been decided on the basis of evidence of knowledge known apart from the seal of confession. The seriousness with which the defense concerning the seal was reviewed is all the more capable of the inference that the common law had received some application of the seal since the trial took place at a time of violent anti-Catholic feelings. Lord Coke would later note the law to be "that the privilege of confession extendeth only to felonies,"[28] basing this opinion on a statute known as *Articuli Cleri* from the reign of Edward II and referring to the trial of Fr. Garnet.[29] The reference is ambigious, for the statute cited does not concern the seal, and Lord Coke's opinion rests solidly on the basis of the argument he made in the *Garnet* case, an argument that contributed nothing to the decision of the case.[30]

[24]2 How. St. Tr. 218 (1606).

[25]See Nolan, "Seal of Confession" at 653.

[26]*Id.*

[27]*Id.*

[28]*Id.* at 652.

[29]*Id.* at 652-653.

[30]*Id.* at 653. For a contemporary accounting of the Garnet case see J. Gerard, *The Autobiography of a Hunted Priest* 263-279 (P. Caraman transl., 1988).

The later post-Reformation evidence points clearly to the conclusion that even if some form of the priest-penitent privilege had been received into the common law of England on the basis of the seal of confession it did not survive the Reformation. The penal laws against the Catholic religion so changed the common law that any vestiges of Catholic privileges or practices were either completely abolished or driven underground. The Civil War would firmly anchor the grip of anti-Catholic bias in English beliefs and practices, and the Glorious Revolution would confirm this grip until the 19th century and, in cases pertaining to the royal family, until the present day.[31] Contemporary English law does not recognize the priest-penitent privilege.[32] However, policy judgment might make it imprudent to call clergy unwilling to testify about matters received in confidence, and judges might still be loathe to compel testimony from priests and other clergy determined to remain silent.

3. *The Priest-Penitent Privilege in the United States*

No jurisdiction in the United States has received into its body of law the priest-penitent privilege on the basis of its existence in the common law of England.[33] By and large the modern rules of evidence have developed in this country independent of the development in post-Reformation England.[34] The law in both countries, however, recognizes an obligation on the part of all individuals to testify concerning relevant facts of which they have knowledge when they are duly called to do so. Exceptions apply in the United States in order to preserve the constitutional right against self-incrimination and also in those cases where the law itself has otherwise recognized an exception by way of privilege, immunity, or incompetency. The only testimonial privilege received directly on the foundation of English common law is the attorney-client privilege, one intimately connected with the judicial process and one's rights against self-incrimination.

[31]Neither the sovereign nor any member of the royal family in line of succession to the throne may embrace the Catholic Church or marry a person who is a Catholic.

[32]See II Halisbury's *Laws of England* ¶464 (4th ed. 1973).

[33]See note 1, *supra*.

[34]In part this is true because the English common law received into the law of the several states is typically the law as it existed at the time of the first permanent English settlement in North American territory later to become the United States. This would be the year 1607, the year of the founding of Jamestown.

In 1813 a New York court was the first American tribunal to allow the priest-penitent privilege. The court allowed the claim of privilege to a Jesuit priest who was unwilling to testify in breach of the seal of confession.[35] The court was sympathetic to the consequences of compelling the priest to violate the obligation of the seal or face punishment for contempt. In admitting the privilege the right of free exercise of religion was cited.[36] The decision rested on this principle *sui generis* despite the lack of common law precedent or any statutory basis for the claim.

A second case arose in New York in 1817.[37] This time the clergyman involved was an ordained Protestant minister. This case was distinguished from that involving the Catholic priest on the basis of no denominational tradition or practice requiring the sacramental confession of sins and no religious obligation similar to the seal of confession. The result was to disallow the claim of privilege, and the minister was ordered to testify. This he did. Partially in reaction to this second case and the distinctions the decisional law had made between Catholic and Protestant parties the New York legislature enacted the first statute in the United States dealing with the priest-penitent privilege. This law of 1828 provided:

> No minister of the gospel or priest of any denomination whatsoever, shall be allowed to disclose any confession made to him in his professional character, in the course of the discipline enjoined by the rules or practice of such denomination.[38]

Since 1828 the New York statute has been the basis for similar enactments in virtually all the states. Furthermore, the general

[35]*People* v. *Phillips* (N.Y. Ct. Gen. Sess. 1813), abstracted unofficially 1 *Western L.J.* 109 (1843), quoted in Privileged Communications to Clergymen, 1 *Cath. Law.* 198 (1955).

[36]See Privileged Communications to Clergymen, 1 *Cath. Law* at 207:

> It is essential to the free exercise of a religion that its ordinances should be administered–that its ceremonies as well as its essentials should be protected. The sacraments of a religion are its most important elements... Secrecy is of the essence of penance. The sinner will not confess, nor will the priest receive his confession, if the veil of secrecy is removed: To decide that the minister shall promulgate what he received in confession, is to declare that there shall be no penance; and this important branch of the Roman Catholic religion would be thus annihilated.

[37]*People v. Smith, N.Y. City Hall Rec.* 77 (1817).

[38]*N.Y. Rev. Stat.* 1828, Pt. 3, c. 7, tit. 3 §72.

tendency has been toward an expansion of the terms of the privilege so that each religious body is treated on equal terms, even those not clearly spelling out a policy of confession or confidentiality.[39] This has been to the benefit of individuals and clergy of all faiths and denominations in the resulting practice of looking at the privilege from the perspective of public policy favoring access to the clergy for confidential exchanges, regardless of denominational policy concerning confession. Four indicators have been used to justify the expansion of the priest-penitent privilege: 1) communication originates in a setting that entails the keeping of confidences received; 2) confidentiality is viewed as essential to the satisfactory relationship between the parties; 3) the relationship between the parties is one that is sedulously fostered by the community; and 4) injury from any disclosure of the confidences would be seen as greater than any benefit to be obtained by compelling disclosure.[40]

Today virtually all American jurisdictions have enacted statutes setting forth the terms of a privilege of confidential communications between members of the clergy and individuals seeking their counsel or sacramental administrations. The specifics of these statutes vary from state to state, and some do offer more protection than others.[41] There remain, however, a number of critical areas that deserve specific attention.

4. Pastoral Confidentiality and Non-ordained Ministers

Without much doubt the existing "priest-penitent privilege" statutes act to protect the seal of confession from intrusion by the civil power. Looking back, it is clear that the seal has been the motivating factor in the historical development of the privilege in American law. Equally clear is that many of the laws explicitly recognize the value to society when the privilege is extended beyond the sacramental forum of penance. This recognition also rests upon the more widely held religious convictions that confidentiality is an essential aspect of the ability of in-

39For discussion on the recognition of confidentiality as an important component of pastoral practice among various denominations and faiths see Yellin," The History and Current Status of the Clergy-Penitent Privilege," 23 *Santa Clara L. Rev.* 95, 126-137 (1983).

40See 8 Wigmore, *Evidence* ¶2396 (McNaughton rev. ed. 1961).

41See Donna Krier Ioppolo's article in this book.

dividuals to approach their religious leaders with freedom.[42] Thus the general proposition can be made about the current status of the privilege in this country: communications received in pastoral counseling, spiritual direction, and sacramental ministrations, provided they are committed in an atmosphere of confidentiality to *a member of the clergy,* are privileged. The clergy status of the religious leader becomes a matter of real concern, especially in the Catholic community.

In 1971 a member of a religious community of women within the Catholic Church risked contempt of court when she refused to testify in a murder trial concerning matters related to her by the accused.[43] This took place in New Jersey where the relevant law provided:

> (A) clergyman, minister or other person or practitioner authorized to perform similar functions, of any religion shall not be allowed or compelled to disclose a confession or other confidential communication made to him in his professional character, or as a spiritual advisor in the course of the discipline or practice of the religious body to which he belongs or of the religion which he professes.[44]

Sister Margaret claimed the privilege of silence recognized under the terms of this statute because she understood her relationship to the accused to have been one of trust and confidence. She had been a spiritual director and counselor to the defendant for a number of years. In rejecting the claim the court indicated that the issue was one of what was authorized by the Catholic Church:

> Sister Margaret did not, and obviously could not, show that she was a person or practioner authorized to perform functions similar to those performed by a clergyman or minister–more specifically, by a priest. . . . Counsel has been unable to find anything in Catholic doctrine or practice that would give Sister Margaret a right to claim the priest-penitent privilege.[45]

[42]See Yellin, supra note 39, at 126ff.
[43]*In re Murtha,* 115 N.J. Super. 380, 279 A.2d 889 (1971).
[44]*N.J. Stat. Ann.* §2A: 84A-23 (1976).
[45]279 A.2d at 892.

In addition to the court's rejection of her claim was the advice that had been given all along by the religious community's superiors, the woman had no basis for remaining silent from the standpoint of Catholic faith or religious profession of vows.

A reasonable interpretation of this case, *In re Murtha,* is not that only priests are entitled to claim the privilege, but that the Catholic Church does not back the claim of someone other than a priest. Without institutional support from her own religious body the sister's claim was denied. The decision is legally correct, but it is factually mistaken in the view it takes of Catholic doctrine or practice, particularly as it might be articulated by a perspective taken today. Assuming Sister Margaret was legitimately related to the accused as his spiritual director, she had every right in Catholic practice to expect support from the officials of her Church. With that support she should have won her claim.[46]

A fair interpretation of many of the existing priest-penitent privilege statutes suggests that they could be extended to encompass the claims of non-ordained ministers serving within the Catholic Church as pastoral counselors or spiritual directors. These claims would be even stronger if there were greater consensus about what ministry of the laity is, as well as what qualifies one for ministry apart from ordination.[47] These issues are for specification on the level of the local church, particularly by the bishops, pastors, and institutional administrators who employ and supervise most lay ministers. Even apart from consensus and specification, however, the tradition gives consistent testimony to the practice of spiritual direction by non-ordained people, as well as to the development of the seal of confession out of the longer tradition of pastoral discretion. Today we are seeing the rise of a class of professional ministers outside the ranks of the clergy. Many of them are doing things that yesterday might have been totally the prerogative of the priests, yet things that are not intrinsically related to orders but to competence. There is no reason to accept a situation in which Sister Margaret's parishioner's secrets

[46]See Stake, "Professionalism and Confidentiality in the Practice of Spiritual Direction," 43 *The Jurist* 214 (1983).

[47]See discussion on the issue of the laity in the ministry in Georgia Masters Keightley, "Women's Issues are Laity Issues," August 6-13, 1988 *America* 77.

are broken, while Father Smith's parishioner's secrets are kept even when committed outside the seal of confession.[48]

5. *Abrogation of Confidentiality in Child Protection Cases*

In recent decades every American jurisdiction has enacted some type of legislation that seeks to remedy the abuse and neglect of children.[49] Many of the laws provide for the mandatory reporting to designated governmental offices of cases of suspected child abuse or neglect. Some of the states specify that persons belonging to certain professions or occupations are "mandated reporters." Under penalty of law these persons must report every case of suspected child endangerment. Some states identify clergy as mandated reporters. In these situations the priest-penitent privilege is seemingly abrogated by specific legislation. Other statutes do not include the clergy in the lists of mandated reporters, and others clearly exempt the clergy from an obligation imposed upon other professionals or upon the population in general.

Another provision of these laws in some of the states is one which requires members of the clergy to give evidence concerning what they know about allegations of child abuse or neglect, even when what they know was learned under circumstances normally within the protection of the priest-penitent privilege. Other states have simply abrogated all testimonial privileges in respect to facts concerning child abuse, except, of course, the recognized common law privilege of attorney and client.

A rather flagrant example of the impact of these child protection measures can be seen in a recent case from Florida.[50] Earl Sands, a parishioner of the Reverend John Mellish, a Nazarene minister, was under investigation for the suspected child abuse of his six-year-old daughter. Mellish successfully encouraged Sands to surrender to the authorities. Later the minister was questioned by an assistant state attorney, and Mellish refused to provide any information about his relationship with Sands, claiming,

[48]This is as much an internal issue for the Catholic Church as it is a question of the relationship between religion and secular civil order.

[49]See Cole, "Religious Confidentiality and the Reporting of Child Abuse: A Statutory and Constitutional Analysis," 21 *Columbia J.L. Soc. Prob.* 1 (1987).

[50]*State* v. *Sands,* No. 84-9516 CF (Fla. Cir. Ct., Broward Co. sentencing Feb. 25, 1985).

on Sand's behalf, the privilege of confidentiality under Florida law.[51]

A hearing on the issue rejected the claim, holding that all testimonial privileges had been abrogated in cases involving child abuse or neglect, and sentencing Mellish to 60 days in jail for criminal contempt of court when he continued in silence.[52] Mellish appealed the judgment and was released pending the outcome after spending only one day in custody. Before decision on the appeal, however, the Florida legislature intervened and exempted the priest-penitent privilege from abrogation.[53] The *Mellish* case presented an opportunity for a clear constitutional foundation of the priest-penitent privilege, but the new legislation mooted the case. Until another case like this arises in the courts, the existence and reach of legal protection for pastoral confidentiality remains an issue of policy that is dependent upon legislative action.

6. *Constitutional Basis for the Priest-Penitent Privilege*

The case for the constitutional basis of the priest-penitent privilege is premised upon the right to free exercise of religion guaranteed in the first amendment.[54] The case is also philosophically premised upon a priority of the rights recognized by the free exercise clause over the things prohibited by the establishment clause.[55] While no case has enunciated this constitutional foundation for pastoral confidentiality, the leading federal decision, the one that held the priest-penitent privilege applicable in the federal courts on the basis of the so-called federal common law, provides a starting point.[56]

Mullen v. *United States*[57] was decided in 1959 in the United States Court of Appeals for the District of Columbia Circuit. The

[51]*Fla. Stat. Ann.* §90.505 (West 1979).

[52]Hearings in *State* v. *Sands* on August 31 and September 4, 1984.

[53]*Fla. Stat. Ann.* §415.512 (Harrison's Supp. 1985).

[54]U.S. Const., amend. 1: "Congress shall make no law... prohibiting the free exercise of religion."

[55]The position of this priority is that free exercise of religion is essentially a matter of human rights. Whether the state establishes a religion is not such an issue.

[56]See also the discussion concerning the constitutional foundation for the priest-penitent privilege in Cole, supra note 48, at 35-50.

[57]263 *F.2d* 275 (D.C. Cir. 1959).

question was not decided on constitutional grounds, but on the authority of the federal courts to develop evidentiary rules in the absence of Congressional limitations. The court looked to the history of the seal of confession, [58] recognized the way in which the law was developing in the states, and subjected the case to the analysis of Wigmore's teaching concerning the appropriate cases in which the law should recognize exceptions to the general rule that all should give evidence when called.[59]

The first hurdle was to depart from what was considered the settled state of the common law, a state taken to be against admitting the priest-penitent privilege. Here the court was emphatic, "When reason and experience call for recognition of a privilege which has the effect of restricting evidence the dead hand of the common law will not restrain such recognition."[60] Then the court went on to say:

> Sound policy–reason and experience–*concedes to religious liberty* a rule of evidence that a clergyman shall not disclose on a trial the secrets of a penitent's confidential confession to him, at least absent the penitent's consent.[61]

"Reason and experience" are critical factors in this opinion, for in the method of common law adjudication the inquiry proceeds to the recognition of religious liberty as something to which the law will grant concessions. The concession is one that policy arguments to the contrary, presumably everyone that could be thought of under the facts of the case, would not overcome. Along this line there is just a short step to constitutional adjudication, for what religious liberty entails is nothing other than the domain of personal rights protected by the free exercise clause.

Something else is involved here, the mention of which will conclude the discussion. The court located the source of the claim to privilege in the penitent. Catholic tradition, in both ascetical and sacramental practice and in moral theology,[62] roots the pro-

[58]The court relied heavily on the Nolan article first cited in note 16, *supra.*

[59]See note 40, *supra.*

[60]263 *F.2d* at 279.

[61]*Id.* at 280.

[62]See, e.g., 2 Slater, *A Manual of Moral Theology for English-Speaking Countries* 175 (5th rev. ed. 1925):

> The obligation of the seal is imposed in favour of the penitent; it is the penitent's secret, but he himself is not bound by it.

tection of pastoral confidentiality in the care the Church must have for its members and for their security. Thus the constitutional case for protection should not be sought in claims that ministers or religions have for the privilege in their own right. Rather, each individual has, in the dignity of his or her own person, the right to the free exercise of religion, the freedom to pursue God in the silence of one's own room and in the secrets of one's own heart.[63] The Church's mandate must be to foster the protection of this silence and the avenues the Christian heritage has offered in assisting individuals to benefit from it fully. Anything that would betray this mandate and weaken the pastoral concern for confidentiality is to be resisted with full institutional attention. If this means enlisting the secular power in such way that it would impose sanctions upon those who breach pastoral confidences, even in addition to those that might be imposed by ecclesial authority, then so be it.[64]

[63]A teaching developed out of the Sermon on the Mount could support the need for confidentiality as an aid to the type of prayer that Jesus enjoined at Matthew 6: 5-6.

[64]This matter raises the issues of civil and criminal liability for breach of pastoral confidentiality, an issue beyond the scope of this piece. But see *Edwards* v. *St. Stephens Episcopal Church,* No. 844020 (Cal. Super. Ct., San Francisco Co. filed Aug. 5, 1985) (Tort claim against clergyman for alleged breach of confessional secrecy); *Tenn. Code Ann.* §24-1-206 (d) (1980) (Criminal penalty of up to $50 and jail or workhouse imprisonment for up to 6 months for violating pastoral confidentiality).

Practical Addendum on Policy-Making

MARIE BREITENBECK, O.P.

There is, in the canonical tradition, a respect for confidentiality in both oral and written communications, and legislation governing actions to be kept confidential, as well as legislation governing who is bound to confidentiality and to what extent. So, there is wisdom to having policies in place on various actions and responsibilities pertaining to confidentiality within religious institutes and the local church.

In light of what has been said about confidentiality in written and oral communications, policy development might well address the following topics: diocesan statements pertaining to cases of alleged child abuse; protection, management, accessibility, and retention of archives; chancery procedures; curial appointments and fulfillment of duties; maintenance and destrucion of personnel files; guidelines for candidates seeking entrance into religious institutes; guidelines on issues of non-admission to either renewal of profession or perpetual profession; guidelines explaining and facilitating internal governance; criteria for marriages celebrated secretly; tribunal guidelines affecting personnel and procedures.

In developing the actual policy, certain key areas should be addressed.

I. If there is *NO* policy governing a particular issue involving questions of confidentiality of either written or oral communications, should there be one? If so, who are the best resource persons to write a policy?

II. If there *IS* a policy:

A. Is it being followed?

B. What specific issue is being addressed?

C. What is the scope of the policy?

1. If files are involved, what are the selection, access, retention and destruction guidelines of the policy?
2. If the files are subpoenaed, how are subpoenas to be handled and by whom?

3. Are any waivers or consent forms required by this policy? If so, what is to be included in such forms and how are the forms presented to the proper canonical authorities?
4. Are any signatures required, either of person(s) to whom the policy applies or canonical authorities or both? Do such signatures need to be witnessed?
5. Are any warnings to be given regarding the cessation of confidentiality or divulgence of information. Is the warning to be given verbally as well as in writing?
6. Are there any periods of time involved pertinent to addressing this specific issue?
7. Are any oaths administered and, if so, by whom?
8. Are there Vatican or NCCB directives to be taken into account by this policy?
9. Are there any civil law ramifications affecting implementation or non-implementation of the policy?
10. Are there any canonical penalties involved in non implementation of the policy?
11. Are there any exceptions to the policy? If so, what are they and under what conditions and by whose authority are exceptions allowed?
12. Under whose authority is the policy promulgated?
13. How is the policy promulgated so that those who should know the policy do in fact know it?

D. How does the policy implement canon law? Specific references to canons should be given. e.g. "Pursuant to canon...", or "Under the provisions of canon...", or "Having addressed the permission required in canon...." Specific references to the authority of the canonical superior should be included, such as, "By the power invested in me as bishop of...", or "Officialis or..." or as the major superior of...."

E. To whom does the policy apply? Is the policy narrow as to the persons to whom it applies, such as the guidelines for a petitioner and respondent to review testimony in a marriage nullity investigation, or more sweeping, as in cases of alleged child abuse, in which the policy could include numerous persons, e.g. diocesan priests, priest members of religious communities, religious brothers and sisters, transitional and permanent deacons, lay employees and volunteers?

F. Who implements the policy? It must be stated clearly who has the authority to implement this policy, such as the diocesan bishop, vicar general, archivist, officialis, major superior, chancellor, administrative officer of the curia, team, e.g. diocesan bishop in collaboration with civil lawyers or major superior and general council. If a team, committee or council is involved in implementation:

1. who makes the final decision in a given situation?
2. if consent or counsel is required in the policy, is it clearly indicated?

G. What are the canonical consequences of non-implementation? The policy should state clearly:

1. if there is to be a warning given and by whom;
2. if there is to be a hearing, who will preside and who will be present;
3. if there is to be a transfer, who authorizes it;
4. if there is to be a dismissal, by whom and in what manner;
5. if there is a request turned down because of failure to follow policy, how is this rectified?
6. could the canonical consequences of non-implementation give rise to civil law consequences such as a lawsuit?

H. What recourse is available and how does a person go about seeking such recourse? The policy should name persons within a religious institute or diocese whom one has access for the specific purpose of seeking recourse, include policies and procedures for seeking recourse and establish the avalable time involved in seeking such recourse.

CONTRIBUTORS TO *CONFIDENTIALITY*

Marie Breitenbeck, O.P. is a judge on the Court of Appeals for the Province of Atlanta. She holds advanced degrees in theology and psychology and a doctorate in canon law from The Catholic University. She has been a member of the Canon Law Society since 1975, has served on the Board of Governors and committees within the Society, contributed to *Marriage Studies* and was a presenter of the CLSA's workshop on "Confidentiality in Canon Law and Civil Law."

James A. Coriden, is Vice President for Academic Affairs, Academic Dean and professor of canon law at the Washington Theological Union, Washington, D.C. He holds a doctorate in canon law from the Gregorian University and a J.D. from The Catholic University. He has served on the CLSA Board of Governors and has served as editor of a number of Canon Law Society publications.

Donna Krier Ioppolo is Program Director at the Center for Church/State Studies, DePaul University College of Law. She holds an advanced degree in industrial relations and a J.D. from Loyola University, Chicago. She was a presenter of the CLSA's workshop on "Confidentiality in Canon Law and Civil Law."

Elissa Rinere, C.P., is a judge and defender of the Bond of the Tribunal of Hartford, CT and on the Court of Appeals for the Province of Hartford. She holds a doctorate in canon law from The Catholic University, Washington, D.C. As a member of the Canon Law Society of America she has presented workshops, served on committees, and presented a seminar on tribunal ministry at the 1988 annual convention.

Ronald P. Stake is a presbyter of the Archdiocese of Chicago and a member of the Illinois Bar. He holds graduate degrees from the University of St. Mary of the Lake and the University of Cambridge in addition to his J.D. from DePaul University, Chicago.